The Lost Villages

A history of the Holmwoods

Kathy Atherton

Published by Kathy Atherton
© 2008 Kathy Atherton

First published in 2008

British Library Cataloguing in Publication Data

Atherton, Kathy
The Lost Villages: a history of the Holmwoods
   1. Title

ISBN 978-0-9560766-0-1

Printed by the MPG Books Group in the UK

Front cover: Holmwood Common and mill: *detail from a mid-19th century watercolour by ET Wickham;* St Mary Magdalene, South Holmwood: *drawing of 1838 dedicated to Mary Ann Arnold and the subscribers by the architect John Burges Watson (Reproduced by permission of Surrey History Centre)*

Back cover: South Lodge, Betchets Green Cottage, Anstiebury Farm and Wymbletons.

Frontispiece: St Mary Magdalene from Betchets Green: *mid-19th century watercolour by ET Wickham (Reproduced by permission of Surrey History Centre)*

This book has been more than five years in the research and could not have been completed without the help and support of numerous people. I would like to record my gratitude to the staff and volunteers of Dorking Museum, Surrey History Centre, Surrey Archaeological Society, Arundel Castle archives, the National Archive and the Museum of London. In particular I must single out Mary Turner, curator at Dorking Museum, (and the volunteers for supplying copious amounts of tea!), Heather Warne, archivist at Arundel, and Mary Day, (who has been unfailingly generous with time and resources from her own 'archive' in Capel), for special thanks. I am also grateful to Martin and Maureen Cole, Peter Camp and Bruce Galley for sharing their researches with me and to the many organisations and individuals who have kindly allowed me to reproduce illustrations, most notably JJ Heath Caldwell, Des Scutt and Eileen Fox.
Which leaves my remarkably tolerant, encouraging and patient family: Richard Fedrick, Don and Betty Attwood, Thomas and Ulysses: thank you.

Contents

The now vanished watering pond at the roadside at South Holmwood with St Mary Magdalene behind. The Holmwood is pitted with man-made ponds, formed to water animals or the remains of clay diggings. *(Surrey Archaeological Society)*

Introduction

The history of the Holmwood villages is inextricably linked to that of the Common - the 'home' wood which became the great 'waste' of the Manor of Dorking. Hunter, herdsman, woodsman, pioneer settler, villager, remote Londoner and palace-building king: each has plundered its resources. To those who settled within its bounds and close by its margins, the Common has provided heat,

Mid-19th century Holmwood Common with the mill and Moor Lodge in the background and a cottage known as the Glade in the foreground. *Painting by ET Wickham. (Reproduced by permission of Surrey History Centre)*

shelter and sustenance. For some it has been the cause of isolation whilst to others, like the felon and the battered suffragette, it has offered refuge. Faith, anger, joy and loss: it has hosted demonstrations of them all.

But the history of the Holmwoods is also that of the road - from the Roman Stane Street to the turnpike and the dual carriageway - for the scattered settlements of the Holmwood were born of the road, growing prosperous on the rich diet of travellers that it provided, only to be finally lost to its demands.

It is not easy to define the Holmwood. Minnickfold, Minnickwood, Moorhurst, Anstie Grange and Kitlands might as easily be defined as part of Coldharbour. Similarly in the north, where, with the flow of Dorking into Chart Down and Goodwyns, it is no longer easy to say where North Holmwood ends and the town begins. I have therefore confined the scope of this book to the settlements in and immediately around the Common. I have encroached into Beare Green and though the Heath family residences in later years looked more to Coldharbour than to Holmwood, I have included them since that family was instrumental in the formation of Holmwood parish and influential within the communities of the Holmwood for a hundred years.

I have called this book 'a' history of the Holmwoods, aware not just of the assessments that I have made as to the significance of matters, but also of the extent to which what I have written has been dependent upon the survival and accessibility of records. I have not been able to consult every archive, and even had I done so there have no doubt been events of more interest and greater significance of which no written records survive than are recorded. In many cases what I have discovered raises more questions than answers. Nor has it been possible to relate in detail the stories of individuals, of families or of individual houses. This book can in no way, therefore, be regarded as 'the' history of the Holmwoods, only as a contribution towards it.

Natural History, prehistory and mythology

Holmwood Common. *Painting by George Edward Collins. (Dorking Museum)*

A broad band of Wealden Clay sweeps across Surrey where the villages of the Holmwood lie. William Cobbett called it 'bottomless clay', and its weight and consistency, with its poor drainage, makes farming difficult. Plenty of legends exist about this clay, not least amusing the one about the man who got his cart stuck in the mud and went to get help, only to find on his return that horse and cart had sunk without trace.

Arrow-heads from Anstiebury and worked flints, such as this one found between Coldharbour Lane and Redlands and now held at Dorking Museum, are evidence of forays by Stone and Bronze Age man into the forest south of Dorking.

Clay favours oak, and so after the last ice age oaks established themselves across the south-east of England - interspersed with beech, ash, yew, juniper and box – creating the great Wealden forest of which the Holmwood was once a part. From these woods early migrant humans cleared dwelling spaces with their flint axes and constructed semi-permanent camps from which to follow game and harvest fruit. In time they began to cultivate plants and to domesticate animals and eventually farming became established to the north of the Holmwood, along the foot of the more easily worked chalk and greensand hills between Reigate and Guildford. There small permanent settlements appeared as generations hewed and burned, carving the woodland into fields and grazing spaces. And from these bases hunting forays were made into the forest where rain percolated slowly through the clay and where dense tree cover prevented the evaporation of surface water so that bog-like conditions prevailed for much of the year.

Settlement within the forest itself came much later. A mile or so west of South Holmwood Anstiebury fort, on the higher, drier, sandier slopes of Leith Hill, is one of a ring around the Weald. Dating from the first or second century BC, its name derives from *Hanstiga* in the - much later - Saxon language[1]. Probably built by farmers who lived in roundhouses on the chalk, growing barley and

---

[1] From *an* and *stig:* 'path for one'. Recorded in Domesday as Hanstega, it became Anestia, Anesty then Anstie.

oats and husbanding their animals, it is not known whether the 'fort' served as market place, ceremonial centre or place of refuge but by the time of the Roman invasion the area was clearly within the domain of people with energy and resources. Storytellers have envisioned these people under attack in 43AD, with the Legion II Augusta marching up through Surrey and engaging them in battle at Anstiebury. Modern historians consider it unlikely, however, that the Emperor Claudius made his incursions into Britain from the south-east.

With the Romans came the first of Holmwood's great roads. 'Stoney-street', as it was known for centuries by way of comparison with its appalling successors across the Weald, was not built for whatever scattered peoples inhabited the area in the first century: it enabled supplies to be brought up from the coast at Chichester (Noviomagus) to Southwark where there was a bridge across the Thames, thereby connecting the newly established London with the territories of friendly tribes of Britons to the south. Skirting to the east of Leith Hill and to the west of Box Hill in avoidance of the worst of their slopes, it kept to rising ground to escape the Wealden wetness, passing through what were to become Minnickwood, Moorhurst, Anstie Grange and Folly Farms into Redlands Wood, then across Redlands Farm behind the Norfolk Arms at Mid Holmwood and over Holmwood Farm to edge North Holmwood from whence it continued north towards Epsom. It has been suggested that crop marks off Anstie Grange Lane, a stone's throw from the line of the road, might indicate the foundations of a small wayside villa there; certainly, pieces of tile have been found nearby.

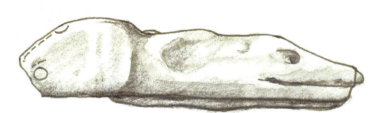

A Romano-British clasp knife with a copper-alloy handle in the shape of a hound's head was found at North Holmwood, close to Stane Street, in 1991.

Likely to have been constructed from the north southwards, as the construction materials could not otherwise have been brought into the boggy Holmwood, Stane Street was in use for three hundred years. It had little lasting effect, however, and today nothing can be seen of the structure; its flints, local sandstone and pebbles have been pillaged and overfilled with clay, its route long since put to the plough. Even a section excavated by the archaeologist SE Winbolt at Redlands Wood in 1935[2], and which was restored to its original condition, re-covered with turf and marked with iron posts, can no longer be identified. Huge numbers of its flints were turned up in 1971, however, on construction of the dual carriageway across Holmwood Farm.

Though it is likely that the road continued in use after the Roman withdrawal at the beginning of the fifth century it soon fell into neglect. Shortly afterwards there was an influx of Germanic peoples into Britain, the 'Anglo-Saxons' who settled over the greater part of Surrey. The Romano-Britons either integrated with them or were forced west, and it is from their language that the name Holmwood derives. The words *ham* and *wudu*, meaning 'home' and 'wood', together make the distinction between the managed wood close to the little

---

[2] Other excavations have taken place: at Folly Farm in 2003 and at Stanecroft in North Holmwood in 1975 and 1984.

settlement at Dorking – which was established in the seventh or eighth century - and the great wood or *weald*[3].

From that fledgling settlement swine herdsmen and cattle drovers made incursions into the 'home' wood, spending their summers in its pastures. There they erected temporary dwellings as their animals fed on beech mast and acorns and in time a semi-permanent seasonal settlement grew up at Ewekene (as Capel was known before the establishment of a chapel there). Hut became homestead and herdsman became farmer: Ewekene became a permanent settlement. And where the drovers went, tracks were established. Between the arable and meadow land that lay close about *Dorchingas* and its remote outlier the woodland grew less dense and impenetrable, transmuting into a patchwork of scrub, grove and grassland in which the Saxons foraged, took wood and hunted.

In the early ninth century the Saxons were threatened in their turn by invading Norsemen and there have been attempts to claim involvement for Holmwood in historical events of this period. It has been suggested that when King Aethelwulf of the West Saxons defeated the Danes at the Battle of Aclea in 853, he camped first at Anstiebury, the battle taking place in what is now Ockley. Some writers even claim that the great victory against the 'heathen' took place there with the ghosts of ancient warriors still to be seen. *"You might see there the warriors, thick as the ears of corn, charging upon either hand, and rivers of blood rolling away the heads and limbs of the slain,"* wrote Henry of Huntingdon in the twelfth century, going on to imagine a rousing Shakespearean scene. *"The Vale of Holmesdale/Never wonne ne ever shall,"* proclaimed William Camden in his late sixteenth century 'Britannia'.

Academic opinion is against these claims. The whereabouts of the battle of Aclea has never been satisfactorily established but Ockley is now considered an unlikely candidate, making the Anstiebury connection implausible. The attentions lavished upon this little edge of the Holmwood by chroniclers over the centuries would appear to have been misguided.

---

[3] Holmwood was given any number of spellings: *Homwude*; *Homwode*; *Homewod*. With the later adoption of 'Holm' - from the Middle English for holly – the distinction between the 'home' wood and the wild Weald has been lost.

After the Conquest - Foreignburgh and the great 'waste'

The system of land administration that was to govern activity in the Holmwood for a thousand years came into being during the late Saxon period when *Dorchingas* and its 'home' wood were owned by Queen Edith, widow of Edward the Confessor and sister of King Harold. After the Conquest her holdings passed to the Conqueror and thence to William de Warenne who had come over from Normandy with him[4]. The shape of de Warenne's Manor of *Dorchingas* reflected the development of the Saxon settlement and its outlying herdsmen's summer dwellings, stretching through the woodland down to Ewekene. It was bounded on the east by the Manors of *Beechworth* and *West Beechworth*, (which also came to be held by the de Warennes), and on the west by the Manors of Milton, *Westgate* (Westcott) and Ockley.

Norman settlements were organised socially and economically around the manor and run by the lord. Some of de Warenne's Dorking lands were worked by labourers who were virtually slaves whilst other land was granted to freeholders who held without obligation. Between the freeholders and the serfs were the small-holders who worked for hire but who also worked some land of their own and who grazed their animals in the Manor's woodland.

This woodland was not as dense as once it had been. The foraging of scores of pigs, as recorded by Domesday, thinned the underbrush; it was plundered for berries and hunted by the Lord for game; wood was taken for fuel, for building and for the production of charcoal. Nonetheless the 'home' wood remained isolated. If there were a few dwellings south of Dorking, *'in bosco de la Homwode juxta Dorkyng'*, it remained largely uninhabited. Settlement was beginning, however: in the neighbouring Manor of Milton Anstiebury Farm, tucked onto the sandier slopes of Leith Hill above the Holmwood, was established before the Conquest.

Domesday records that Anstiebury (*Hanstiga*) was held by one Baldwin in 1086. The current farmhouse was probably built in the early 15th century but has numerous additions.

As populations grew in the following centuries, demand for land increased. So begun the task of taming the heavy clay of the Weald. The Lord made grants of land and a scattering of farms sprang up, fanning down from Dorking and off the drove tracks south. Over the centuries swathes were put to the plough, the woodland parcelled into fields, coppices, and dwelling places. The best positions – dry and with water available, avoiding

---

[4] De Warenne was married to Gundreda, the Conqueror's step-daughter by his wife Matilda; he was later created Earl of Surrey by William II. He based himself in Lewes but the family developed a local base at Reigate Castle.

the worst of the swamps and steep slopes – were cultivated early and the names of many of the early occupants of these farms are recalled even today: Breakspeares, (like Stumbleholt), is recorded in 1281, when it was owned by one Sybil Breakspeare, Bregsells the following year in the ownership of the de Brugeshulle family, Minnickwood in 1381, when it was owned by John Menek, Waterland, (bordering the Common in the Manor of West Betchworth), in 1332, when it was owned by Petere 'ate Watere', and Stubs, (the site of North Holmwood brickworks), in the same year being owned by Ralph and John Stub. Subberies (later Holmwood Park), was granted to Henry Subberye by the Earl de Warenne somewhere between 1278 and 1347.

Settlement probably predates documentary evidence, however. Several place-names bordering the 'home' wood betray their origins as cleared woodland with their roots in pig pasturing: Beare Green takes its name directly from this practise, coming from 'beru', meaning swine pasture. Minnickfold to the west and Henfold to the south probably also have their origins as summer swine pastures whilst *Redelong* (Redlands)[5], *Kyttelond* (Kitlands)[6], *Spokeland* (Spookland), *Blakebrookland*[7] and Waterland indicate land broken in for arable use. The boundaries of these farms, with Inholms, the Lord's great farm which was recorded in 1342, (the very name of which derives from 'nam' meaning seizure, in the sense of taking a piece of land *in* from the ancient woodland[8]), came to define the extent of the remaining 'home' wood.

The settler would usually be granted enough land to keep a family, (which on poor lands would be a greater area than on better soils). Stone was expensive and transport difficult so houses, barns, haylofts and granaries were framed with local timber. Constructed in bays with dung or clay-coated wattle panels, the houses would have had a central, unenclosed fire.

Most of these newly created farms were held on copyholds, a form of landholding abolished in 1925. A copyholder could grant a mortgage on security of his land, but he could not sell, lease or assign it without payment being made to the lord and on his death

The farm at Stumbleholt on the Blackbrook road is mentioned in written records as early as 1281. The earliest part of the house dates from the 17th century when it went by the name of Camdens and was owned, (with neighbouring Woolams - later Wollocks - and Redlands Farm), by Sir George Sondes whose family had built up large holdings in the years after the Black Death. Still farmed in the 18th century when the adjacent Little Stumbleholt was in use as a butcher's shop, the house was purchased in the late 19th century by Edward Charrington of the London brewers, extended and gentrified, becoming known as The Poplars.

---

[5] Redelong/Readeland is mentioned in the court rolls of 1559.
[6] Kyttelond is mentioned in the court rolls in 1437 being owned by John Stapele and his wife Dionisia.
[7] Blakebrookland appears in the court rolls of 1448.
[8] Appearing in records as *Innome, Southinome, Middelinome, Inhomes, Inhamlond, Inhame* and *the Inholmes,* Inholms was let in the 15th century to John Martyn whose descendents tenanted the farm again in the 19th when it was known as Martyn's Farm.

his best beast, (usually a heriot), would be forfeit. Though having similarities with modern-day leases for rent, these feudal land grants were instead (or in addition) made with obligations in terms of labour: occupiers of farms around the 'home' wood were required to load timber and charcoal onto wagons for transport out of the forest, or to manage rogue growth in the valuable woodland.

The woodland was cleared piecemeal, steep rises and areas of poor soil or bad drainage being avoided, leaving small fields with scattered stands of trees and wooded hillsides. The resulting farms were cultivated with difficulty. Stones had to be picked out of the clay. Liming was necessary to neutralize acidity, and though there were chalk hills only a few miles to the north it was not practicable to bring in lime along the narrow swampy lanes that lead to these homesteads with only pack animals for transport. Instead farmers dug marl pits in the corners of their fields, spreading calcareous clay from the lower beds across their land, an arduous undertaking that had to be repeated every two or three years. Even then the soil was difficult to work, being either boggy or too hard to break down and several teams of oxen would have been required for the numerous ploughings required before planting. In dry springs crops shrivelled in the cracked clay, in wet autumns the harvest rotted, and even when cropped, of wheat, barley, oats or rye, the land required long periods of rest. Livestock was important, therefore, and farmers kept cows and sheep. They also exploited their stands of woodland where pigs might forage for beech mast, or amongst the fallen fruit in the orchards and amongst the coppices which provided palings, hurdles, hoops and brooms, whilst root vegetables were grown in farmhouse gardens.

Much of the land to the south of Dorking would never be suitable for farming, however, its slopes too steep, the ground waterlogged or the clay too heavy. When the scramble was over what remained of the Manor's woodland, therefore, were the areas that could not be drawn into economically viable cultivation though it continued to be nibbled away as ever more marginal patches were drawn into use.

By the end of the medieval period the remaining 'home' wood was known as a 'waste' but worthless it was not. The Lord hunted there, took rabbits and harvested it for charcoal, fuel and timber. With reserves of gravel, firewood, bracken, holly, turf, acorns and beech-nuts, wild fruit, and most importantly of all, grass, it was a resource which played a significant role in the economy of the Manor. Rights to take fish for domestic consumption (*piscary*), turf or peat (*turbury*), fallen wood, gorse, holly, bracken and underbrush (*estovers*), to graze grass-eating plough animals (*herbage*), or to forage pigs (*pannage*) on uncultivated manorial land were negotiated between the Lord and his tenants at meetings of the manorial courts. It was in the interests of all that the Common was not abused for there was a shifting co-dependency between the Lord, who gained an income from the grant of rights, and the tenants. In particular the right of herbage was vital to the economics of the Manor for the summer grazing of plough animals on the Common enabled smallholders to grow fodder on their own lands, without which such animals could not survive the winter to carry out their labours on the Lord's lands.

Far from being an open space, therefore, over which nobody exercised control, the use of the Holmwood was vigorously policed. The Lord's bailiff agreed the number of animals that might be grazed, the amount of wood that might be taken, and the area of bracken that might be cut. Supernumerary animals found on the Common were 'impounded' – that is, taken off the Common and put into a pound with a fine being payable for their release, a practice that went on into the twentieth century.

10

In time all this activity had an effect on the landscape for as grazing livestock numbers increased, tree cover diminished. Slowly the home 'wood' became a wood 'common'.

Without really productive land, however, the dwellers of the Holmwood's farms and of the scattered dwellings around the waste – labourers, timber cutters and charcoal burners - were the poor and isolated people of a poor and isolated region. For most the limit of their horizons was Dorking where a twice-weekly market had been established, and where the Lord's business was conducted and all activity on his land regulated. His steward visited the Manor every few weeks and every male member of each household, even from *Foreignburgh* (which borough covered the Holmwood down to Betchets Green) and *Waldburgh* (the Weald borough), had to attend the Court Baron when he came. Though a *'capella'* had been established to the south not long after the Conquest, it was also to Dorking that the people of the Holmwood had to bring their dead. Travel into Dorking would therefore have been a necessity. Travel across the clay, however, has always been a fraught issue.

The Romans' 'stone' street had long since been abandoned, its high-maintenance surface of little use to those who were not bringing goods long distance but criss-crossing from homestead to water source to common grazing. Swine herdsmen, woodsmen and charcoal burners had worn their own tracks through the woods, as had those whose homesteads were established on the higher, sandier lands to the west, away from the quagmire into which the Roman road had dissolved. Where such byways crossed the lower lying clay journeyers must trudge through almost impassable bog. Long-distance travellers therefore avoided the woodlands and the way south from Dorking developed on better drained ground, via Coldharbour, coming down to Ockley from the west. It was a route that increased in significance from the mid-fourteenth century when, at the end of the de Warenne line, the Manor was inherited by Richard Fitzalan, Earl of Arundel, who administered its business from his Sussex base. The track was precipitous and totally unsuitable for wagon carriage. There was, however, little alternative.

This would never have been so apparent as when tenants carried out their duties to transport timber and firewood out of the manorial wood. To the north woodland had all but disappeared by the fourteenth century and the Manor was supplying cartloads of fuel to villages such as Kingston. Though once off the clay there was an adequate road north, moving loads out of the Holmwood up to Dorking was an onerous, and for much of the year an impossible, obligation and Holmwood tenants were regularly fined for not performing their duties. In the 1420s a collective annual fine began to be levied, in effect exempting local men from the service. No payment, however, could exempt them from the need to travel in the centuries to come.

Holmwoodburgh

By the sixteenth century, when Foreignburgh was renamed Holmwoodburgh, the forest south of Dorking had been carved into a patchwork of freeholds and copyhold tenancies. What remained of the 'home' wood was eight hundred acres of commonly grazed woodland, ringed with farms, some of whose farmhouses are inhabited still. With their internal smoke bays rather than open roofs, they were surrounded by barns, granaries, kitchen gardens and orchards.

Bounding the Common to the north were the farms of Goodwyns, Stubs and Rushets. Protridges and Spookland (both eventually incorporated into Holmwood Farm) lay to the north-west. Sand-loving firs clothed the western hillsides of Redlands Farm, the Lord's coppices of Hambrich[9] and Swires, and Maryfields (later Whitehouse now Folly Farm) up to the Coldharbour lane. To the south, from

Morden's map of 1695 shows the route of Stane Street and the settlements at Capel, Newdigate and Ockley. *(Dorking Museum)*

Redlands Farm appears in records in 1559 and has a 16th century house. Owned, like much land in the area, by the Sondes family in the 17th century it was subsumed into Edward Walter's Bury Hill estate in the 18th century. In 1813 it was bought by the Duke of Norfolk. It then passed into the ownership of another of the area's great landowners, the Lee Steeres of Ockley. The Cosins family, who occupied it in the hard years of the early 19th century, emigrated to Canada in 1831.

whence a track meandered to Capel were Wiggons (Betchets Green), Subberies (Holmwood Park), Swites (Holmwood Park Farm), Breakspeares (comprising much of the Brookwood Corner area), and Bregsells (also known as Bromans), with Kitlands lying far to the west. Moorhurst and Trouts fell within the Manor of Ockley. Nyes (Vigo), Anstiebury and much of Maryfields were in pockets of the Manor of Milton that were surrounded by Dorking lands. To the east Wymbletons and Waterland lay against the Common, partly in the Manor of West Betchworth. From these farms plough animals grazed the wood common, the eleven acre waste at Beare Green and the smaller Maynack wood.

---

[9] Hambrich (now Hambridge) survives as part of Redlands Wood which also comprises the wooded western extremities that rise up behind Redlands Farm of which they were once a part.

The cottage at Betchets Green was built in the 1590s when John Symons was granted a small patch of land from the Common on which to keep a few animals. With a smoke-bay at one end, the chimney is a later addition. Its inhabitants feature in the book, 'A Commoner's Cottage', by Frances Mountford.

In 1572 the Duke of Norfolk acquired the Fitzalans' land and titles by marriage. As joint owner of the Manor[10] he benefited from a payment every time a piece of copyhold land changed hands. He also benefited from the service elements in Holmwood tenancies that obliged holders of farms like Inholms to preserve the wood and underbrush on the Holmwood. Though well managed woodlands generated substantial sums from pasturage and pannage, timber, which wood pastures like Holmwood could provide, was much in demand. Fifteen loads of fencing poles were brought out of Holmwood in 1538 for Henry VIII's construction site at Nonsuch Palace in Epsom. (Indeed, much of the wood that was brought up at the King's command from Sussex and south-eastern Surrey would have traversed along the edge of the Common, thirty-six loads of scaffolding poles coming up from Capel, with timber coming from Ewood and Leigh, and from Newdigate and Rusper, where sawpits shaped timber for the palace's great octagonal towers. All this would have travelled with great difficulty and little speed, by cart, along the eastern edge of the Common, coming in directly from Newdigate past Swites or via Lodge or Red Lanes, connected by the - now disused - Brimstone Lane, towards Blackbrook). Iron bloomeries, which had existed in the Weald since Roman times, also competed for fuel as did charcoal burners upon whom blacksmiths were dependent until the coming of the railways made it possible for coal to be transported.

Beside the Common in the Manor of West Betchworth, Waterland Farm has been dendrochronologically dated to 1590 though the farm predates this particular house, the land having been occupied at least since 1332.

---

[10] The original holding had been split in half but was eventually recovered by the Howards in its entirety.

Tiny 16th century timber-framed Cinders Cottage off Mill Road is now tile hung, the front having been remodelled with a bay window and an ornate gable when it became a lodge to Holmwood Park.

By the 1540s deforestation had lead to fuel shortages in London, as a result of which a series of measures was enacted prohibiting the cutting and sale of wood for the iron business on commons close to the city. Luckily for the Holmwood, the foundry at nearby Ewood had plentiful supplies from its own woodland and the prohibitions therefore came in time to afford protection against the degradation that had been suffered by other commons in the vicinity.

By the reign of Elizabeth I everything of value within the Manor had been claimed and regulated. The large farms that had been originally established had been broken down somewhat and medium-sized holdings were now packed tightly along the fringes of the waste. Small grants of an acre or so on which a labourer might keep a few animals were still being made out of the Common, however, tucked onto accessible scraps beside farms and tracks. A number were sandwiched between the 'Holmwood' lane that came down from Dorking via Stonebridge and Rushets; others clustered where the Capel track opened into the waste, with a scattering beside the greens at Holmwood Corner, Minnickwood and Betchets Green. Still others were taken from the Common alongside the track which entered the waste from 'Cleygate Hill' in the north and crossed directly south, away from the Common's edge, creating islands at the Willows, the Oaks and the Elms at what was to become Mid Holmwood. Such plots could not have provided a living to their occupants, who laboured for others or worked at a trade, but access to a small piece of land enabled them to supplement their incomes with a few animals and a vegetable garden.

There were more necessitous of shelter than could pay for land, however, and until 1588 common law allowed a person who could raise a roof with a fire in the hearth between sunrise and sunset to remain in whatever hovel he been able to construct. Many of the modern dwellings situated deep within the Common or where it edged Inholms have their origins in such isolated squatters' dwellings including Eutrie, Brook and Holmwood Lodges, Daisy Lodge (Bellis House), Vine Cottage and Ivy Porch (the White Barn). The inhabitants of these hovels were impoverished, forced to make what living they could taking wood, collecting nuts and berries, charcoal burning, turf cutting, making brooms or hoops, and by poaching. Many were widows.

The squatters were the most obvious combatants in a war between the Lord, those with legitimate rights who would lose out if land was lost or degraded, and those without. In 1649 Robert Fuller, who occupied a squat on the site of Holmwood Lodge, enclosed ten perches 'to the harm of the Lord and tenants'. He was fined and ordered to reinstate. Henry

Ledger, who occupied another taken out of the temporarily 'waste' Inholms, was fined for the same offence. They were but two of many and not all of those appropriating illegally were squatters, either.

Nor was appropriation the only abuse; the wood of the Common was pillaged, both for domestic fuel and to fire the kilns which many farmers now kept in the corners of their fields. These kilns produced lime from chalk which was used to treat the area's poor soils. Demand was such that some set themselves up in business using resources that were not their own: in 1661 Henry Hewlett was fined for having cut thorns and furze on the Common for such use, compounding his offence by selling his product outside the parish. Other offences included the stopping of watercourses - in 1658 Richard Haybittle did so *to the damage of the Lord and tenants'* - and the running of unauthorised animals. In 1676 Henry Gosden of Bakers at the foot of Redlands, together with John Barnster, William Dibble and Edward Hooker, was accused of keeping and pasturing goats, (which were not regarded as 'commonable'), and in 1686 William Sprouten carried away ferns. To prevent such abuses the Duke's agent policed the Common, imposing fines and ordering restitution. Haybittle was ordered to remove his dam; Sprouten was fined two shillings, and the goat-keepers five. The goat problem was a recurring one, however: in 1672 a number of Holmwood men, including Thomas Symons of Betchets Green and Henry Swan of Bregsells, were ordered to remove their animals on pain of a fine of twenty shillings; in 1679 and the following year, too, Edward Hooker pastured goats, being threatened with a £5 fine for the same offence in 1682 and again in 1683 when he was threatened with a fine of £15, a huge sum.

We know much about Holmwood at this time because in 1649 the Earl of Arundel and Sir Ambrose Browne of Betchworth Castle, (owner of the neighbouring manor and a quarter share of the Manor of Dorking), undertook a survey of their Manor. In 1583 when, (under threat of invasion), local men had been required to present themselves in Guildford so that their suitability to fight might be assessed, the borough of Holmwood had been able to supply forty pikemen, billmen, gunners and archers. By the 1660s, according to the Hearth Tax returns, there were a hundred and fifty-three hearths in the Holmwood, equating to a population of several hundred. There was, however, no village either within the 796 acre waste or on its margins in 1649.

The survey records a number of large farmer landowners: Sir George Sondes' 126 acre Redlands was only a part of his estates: he had a similar acreage between Protridges and the Coldharbour lane and smaller holdings at

An early 17th century house lies subsumed under Vigo's later brick façade. Originally in the Manor of Milton the farm was known as Nyes, probably after the Ny family who were living in the area in the late 16th century, and renamed after the Battle of Vigo in 1701.

Camdens (Stumbleholt) and Woolams to the east of the Common and at Garmers Grove between Stubs and Inholms. The Young family of Breakspeares, (which had occupied the farm for at least seventy years), also owned the adjoining Turners, whilst Swites was owned by Thomas Constable who held a hundred acres at Moorers, (Moorhurst in the Manor of Milton), and a large swathe from Beare Green down to Capel. Many of these farms would remain in the same families for many generations: the Bax family, who owned large amounts of land in the adjoining Manor of Ockley, may only have recently acquired Kitlands in 1649, it having previously been in the Constable family, but they would hold it another two hundred years, until 1824. Similarly with East Bregsells: variously spelled *Brigills* and *Burgsills,* in 1589 it had been owned by Robert Swan, whose father had acquired it during the reign of Henry VIII; by 1649 it was owned by Mary Swan and would remain in the family that established Holmwood windmill until the 1850s.

A representation of Holmwood in 1649 showing the farms and a patchwork of smaller holdings. The steep western slopes, running up towards the Coldharbour lane at the top, are heavily wooded (shown green) as are the Lord's coppices of Hambrich, (melding into Redlands in the centre), and Swires (centre left). The 'Cleygate' lane enters the Common from mid right and Nettlefold's pits (yellow edge) are mid left. No track is shown across the Common but there is a cluster of dwellings about the Blackbrook in the area of the Willows and the Oaks at Mid Holmwood suggesting the existence of one. Many of the field and estate boundaries shown are still in place today. The ancient settlements (circled in blue) within the Common nearly all remain with little addition.

The farms were interspersed with a patchwork of smaller holdings. On the east these hugged the Manor boundary, facing onto the open common: Woolams (Wollocks), Camdens (Stumbleholt), Blackbrook, Heathfields and Shernbrooke (Brook Lodge and Scammels).

Waterland and Wymbletons in the Manor of West Betchworth lay against the Common in the south. On the west Harescroft, Bakers, Fosters, Hookes and Isemongers, Rudons and Cowpers nestled at the foot of the great farms that rose up the gentle slopes behind them, the steep western extremities of which were heavily wooded. Some had acquired a portfolio of these smaller holdings: Edward Nettlefold and John Heather held just about everything that ran from Hooke/Isemongers (Redlands Bank) down to Wiggons at Betchets Green and their families had done so since the 1580s at least.

Many of the smaller holdings were home to tradesmen whose activities supported farming. There was a wheelwright, William Hooker, at Betchets Green and in 1658 a blacksmith named William Dudley took on premises where the 'Cleygate' lane entered the Common close by Protridges and Spookland, a business that remained in the family for nearly a hundred years until taken over by a wheelwright in 1748. There was industry too: a large area known as Longepitte, (in what is now South Holmwood, where Norfolk, Buckingham and Warwick Roads are situated), had for three quarters of a century at least been held by the Nettlefolds and was now given over by Edward Nettlefold, (whose name is commemorated in Nettlefold Cottage), to marl diggings.

The period after the restoration has been depicted as one of abundance in the Holmwood. Daniel Defoe, writing in the 1720s, claimed that strawberries were produced in such quantity as to be taken to market by the cartload, and that when James II was Duke of York in the 1670s the largest stags in England were caught on the Holmwood. Whether or not the future king hunted there with the Brownes of Betchworth Castle, (with whom he was certainly close), it is unlikely that the impoverished inhabitants of the Common would have recognised the picture of rural plenty as they struggled with the intractability of the soil and with the isolation it engendered.

That isolation was coming to an end, however, for traffic through the Holmwood was increasing. For generations drovers had driven their beasts along the waste's periphery, tenants from as far away as Billingshurst passing their pigs to London via Dorking. By the late seventeenth century, though, improvements in agriculture had resulted in surpluses in corn from Capel and the surrounding farms being traded and therefore transported. In addition many of the villages around, as far south as Newdigate, Capel, Ockley and even Horsham, raised the five-toed Dorking fowl for which the market

A 17th century cottage with an end chimney, Stoneheal in South Holmwood was known as Tone Heat in the late 18th century when it was leased, with Moor Cottage, to the manager of the Dorking workhouse, Nathanial Wix.

had become famous, necessitating travel across the Holmwood. But for much of the year travel, even on horseback, was nearly impossible for local and long distance traveller alike. The waterlogged tracks that had developed across the Common were, as the Lords' surveyor commented, composed of *'a clay which is so apt to dissolve with any moisture the least rain makes a puddle and after any little continual wet the ways are scarce passable'*. The laden wheels of the wagons that had begun to replace pack horses had a deleterious effect on the roads to west and east, the one via Coldharbour high and narrow, the other, (which had grown up to bring wood and iron out from Ewood and which ran from Chart Lane via the eastern boundary of the Holmwood then along the Manor boundary via Red or Lodge Lanes), low and swampy. Their effect on the track across the Holmwood itself was surely even worse. The only produce easily marketed was that which could be driven on foot.

Wood could not be moved in winter and wheat fetched higher prices in Dorking than it did in Horsham because of the difficulty of getting it there. But the scattered people of the Holmwood and of its surrounding farms had not only to reach the market; they must walk or ride the miles into Dorking to celebrate their marriages[11], to bury their dead and to have their flour milled. They had also to attend Courts Baron and County Court sessions. Criminal trials were held quarterly at different locations within the county and those selected to serve on juries were required to go wherever the court was sitting - as Thomas Symons of Betchets Green was compelled to do in 1662 when he had to make his way to Croydon. Travel was becoming both an obligation and a necessity.

In the medieval period the lord of the manor had been responsible for the highways within his domain but in 1555 responsibility had been transferred to parishes. Now each parishioner between the ages of 18 and 60 earning less than a certain sum per year must labour a certain number of days on the roads - though it was possible to provide a substitute labourer or

Emmanuel Bowen's map of Surrey c1745 shows a well developed track through the Holmwood as well as the Coldharbour and Newdigate roads. References in the 1649 survey to copyholds in the Mid Holmwood area suggest that by that date the track had been established.

---

[11] To the extent that lowlier people ever consecrated their marriages in church prior to the Marriages Act of 1735.

to pay a sum of money in lieu. Those with an income in excess of the stipulated sum were required to provide a man, a horse and a cart rather than to work themselves. Finance for the required stones and chippings came from the commuted payments of those who did not labour and from fines for non-performance. There was usually little money, however, for other than keeping back the undergrowth and filling in holes in the key routes.

The tracks winding up over the Holmwood, linking homestead with water source

and grazing would have seen little, if any, attention with even the main routes impassable for much of the year. The central track over the Holmwood, however, was growing in importance, if not reliability. In July 1662 the Court Session Rolls reported that: *'the highway at the south end of the Homewood, leading from Dorking to Capel has been so out of repair.... that the King's liege people cannot pass without great danger, to their common nuisance.'* It was recommended that: *'the inhabitants of Dorking ought to make repair to the same whenever necessary.'* For the inhabitants of the towns and villages of the Weald the Holmwood was a barrier to their way north. Their resources remained inaccessible to the growing London markets, their wood – lying by the roadside all winter - unsaleable. Something would have to be done.

The 17th century Nutcracker Cottage on Spook Hill was built close to the edge of the Common near to rising springs long before the establishment of Spook Hill on to which it backs. In later centuries a cluster of dwellings grew up nearby. Known as Little Egypt, the rest were swept away with the building of the Studio and Sefton Villas whilst the cottage became a laundry in the early 20th century when it was known as Royston.

The great farm at Inholms

Established as early as 1342, the 200 acre Inholms was tenanted in the 15[5h] and 16th centuries but by the 17th century it was 'waste'. The 1649 survey plan shows unauthorised dwellings having been carved out of it. Difficulty in letting it persisted: in the 1740s it was still untenanted and in *'bad condition'*, the house *'almost useless'*, perhaps the reason that the Duke allowed John Constable of Brookmeadow - a smallholding taken out of the Common on the Black Brook - to carve a piece out of it for the planting of fruit trees in the 1670s. By the 19th century Inholms had been acquired by the Hopes of the Deepdene (together with which it was inherited by the Duke of Newcastle). In mid-century the farmhouse (Old Inholms) beside the Common not far from Ivy Porch was abandoned and a new one built on the Blackbrook road. That house was sold off in the 1950s, however. The name Inholms is now in use by the farm once known as Wollocks on the eastern side of the Blackbrook road whilst the original farm has been split into two: Old Inholms and Beldams.

The turnpike - smugglers, thieves and vagabonds

' *Over the whole Wild of Kent and Sussex it is the same,'* wrote Daniel Defoe in 1724: *'the corn is cheap at the barn because it cannot be carried out, and dear in the market because it cannot be brought in'.* Holmwood was no exception: in 1752 the Coldharbour track was described as a *'shocking, steep ravine, quite impassable for wheels'.* Holmwood exemplified the choice all over the Weald, to keep to the drier ridges with all the attendant difficulties of steep slopes, or to become enmired in clay bog, as was the route to

Rocque's map of 1765 shows the new turnpike passing above Nutcracker Cottage, across the Common then down to edge it again from the Nag's Head south. 'Mid Holmwood', set about the Black Brook which had higher water levels in this period than in the present day, was the most populous area of the Common

Newdigate. So bad was the problem that for much of the year it was impossible, claimed the landowners of Horsham in their petition to Parliament in support of the establishment of a new road, for them to reach London save via Canterbury. The roads, they claimed: *'by reason of the soil thereof and of many heavy carriages frequently passing the same, are become so ruinous and bad, that in the winter season some parts thereof are almost impassable for any manner of carriages and very dangerous for loaded horses and travellers, and in many parts too narrow, as to render the same very incommodious and dangerous to passengers; and in regard the said roads cannot be amended and kept in repair.'*

In 1755 the Horsham and Epsom Turnpike Act passed through Parliament and a new road came into being, the route of which would change the Holmwood forever.

Running through Capel, Dorking and Mickleham to 'Ebisham', (with a spur to Ockley to connect into the route to Arundel[12]), the turnpike was constructed and maintained by trustees - the Evelyns of Wotton,

---

[12] A less important route than once it had been since the Howards now based themselves in Worksop and London.

the Howards of the Deepdene, the Steeres of Ockley and scores of landowners who stood to benefit from the alleviation of the woeful situation. Borrowing against future tolls from which they would recoup construction and maintenance costs they widened, levelled, and, in the case of the stretch between Dorking and Capel, constructed a route across the clay.

The road ran out of South Street, down the 'flint' hill, across the Bents Brook and onto the Common. Avoiding the springs and streams on the lower lying land there it climbed up to where North Holmwood church now stands. From there it rose steeply to the twenty-five mile post, following the line of the established track over the Common then downhill to 'Mid Holmwood'. It is for this reason that the older cottages to the east of Spook Hill have their backs to the modern road for they faced the turnpike. From 'Mid Holmwood' it edged between Common and farmland to join the established route from Beare Green to Capel. There was a tollgate (Harrow gate) near Dorking, at the junction with Hampstead Road[13], and another (Holmwood gate) just before the twenty-seven mile post at Holmwood Corner.

Travellers on foot were exempt from tolls, though they might be charged for baggage. One shilling and sixpence was payable for a coach pulled by up to 6 horses, a shilling for a coach pulled by up to four horses and sixpence for one pulled by one or two horses, acknowledging the wear caused by heavy vehicles. Wagons and carts paid a shilling, laden animals were charged two pence, droves of cattle ten pennies per score and calves or sheep five pennies per score[14].

Use of the road was dictated by the season, however, for the surface was a churned up mud-bath in winter with baked clay ruts in dry summers, passable on foot or horseback but almost impossible for wheeled vehicles. As late as the 1820s William Cobbett reported pitifully slow progress along the turnpike and across the Common. '*It is all clay here,*' he said. Indeed for local traffic just reaching the turnpike was sometimes impossible in winter so parlous was the state of local roads. The quagmire near Holmwood's mill in the early nineteenth century was a hazard to grazing cows whilst the swamp that was Inholms Lane – still the responsibility of the parish - consumed scores of cartloads of gravel and required ploughing to level it. It would be many years before technology overcame the difficulties of the clay, and if the rises of the turnpike were difficult the descents could be treacherous: in 1777 a servant of Peter King died under the wheels of a wagon and in the same year a man working for Edward Payne of Sussex was run over by a fish cart. In both cases the wagon and horses responsible for the deaths were forfeited.

Finding itself in prime position at the roadside the late 17th century Old Nag's Head was converted to an inn sometime before 1799 when it was occupied by a widow named Elizabeth Wood of Dorking. In business until about 1830, it stands next to the stuccoed September Cottage facing the road at Mid Holmwood where the Black Brook drains down from Redlands Wood. By the early 19th century it was surrounded by dwellings and orchards.

---

[13] Later it was moved south to just past the Bush Inn
[14] The parishes made a contribution, Dorking initially paying £15 a year, rising to £20 in 1805 and £25 in 1814.

21

In 1775 Messrs Borer Briggs, Snelling and Ede from Leigh were fined £3 for avoiding payment at the Holmwoodgate. The new road was not built to benefit local labourers, however: it connected Dorking to the coast and the territories between with greater efficiency than had been possible at any time since the Roman period. And at the Dorking Gap the North Downs chalk ridge was penetrable, allowing passage to London. Landowners from a wide area reaped the benefits: wood and corn could be carried up from Sussex; pigs, sheep and cows could be driven along its route. And access to market brought an increase in prosperity to farms in the vicinity enabling landowners to increase rents.

It brought other opportunities. Wheelwrights and blacksmiths came to trade all along the route: in South Holmwood, at Blackbrook (the Plough), at the Norfolk Arms, at Rosewood Cottage, next to Protridges and latterly at Spring Cottages. And by 1799 one of a couple of cottages set within the Common where the road emerged downhill just south of Mid Holmwood Lane had been converted into an inn. Providing food, accommodation and stabling, it became known as the Nag's Head.

The Nag's was soon joined by the Duke's Head – a converted sixteenth century cottage at Beare Green - and the White Hart - established by Joseph Turner on land leased from Bregsells. A beershop was established on the Blackbrook road and another, early in the next century, opposite the new mill. Probably catering for locals rather than the road trade it was run by a carpenter, Edward Pledge, and became known as the Sawyers' Arms on account of its proximity to the nearby sawpits, one next to the turnpike gate and another enclosed illegally by Thomas Holland near the mill. A timber yard occupied the site of Spring Cottages. There wood was prepared for the roadside wheelwrights, for building and for carriage out of the Holmwood for the timber of Holmwood's heavily wooded western hillsides was a valuable crop: when the Duke of Norfolk bought Redlands, Anstie and Folly farms from the Bury Hill estate in 1813 he paid £12,000, more than half the value of the farms, for their timber. By the mid-nineteenth century the Sawyers' was also servicing the road with its own brewery, bedrooms and a pin alley.

The road also made it less difficult – at least for part of the year – to get corn in, and flour out, of Holmwood's higher reaches. Though established by the 1760s, it was not until 1772 that Henry Swan was granted a licence for his post-mill - with its sails mounted on a brick roundhouse - to occupy an elevated site between Four Wents and the turnpike. Visible from the turnpike and Blackbrook road, it was surrounded by farms, (not least Swan's own at Bregsells).

A track already ran into the Common from Wymbletons – there were ancient cottages scattered within the Common and the Four Wents junction was

Part of Edward Mogg's 1817 map of the road from London to Worthing showing the Holmwood stretch of the turnpike and the Nag's Head. *(Dorking Museum)*

already so named – and the development of this track enabled corn to be brought in from the east as well as from the west. It became known as Mill Lane (now Road) and it opened up the interior of the Common, in effect establishing a new southern boundary. The years after the establishment of the mill also saw the area beside the turnpike between Folly Farm and Betchets Green grow industrious and populous with clay diggings, sawpits, a brewhouse, and a small chapel.

Henry Swan, who established Holmwood's mill, served as Overseer of the Poor and Surveyor of the Highways whilst his Quaker family ran nearby Bregsells. His millers kept cows, fowl and pigs and by the mid-19th century the mill was a substantial business with orchards, a dairy and a brew-house. There were also clay pits and kilns for brick-making, a well-stocked haberdashery and, possibly, a laundry. The mill remained in the family until Swan's great-grandson emigrated to America in the 1860s. (*Dorking Museum)*

More than likely it was proximity to the turnpike that allowed George Miller of Dorking's Ram Alley pottery to begin production to the north of the Common in 1795. His house and kilns stood between Benson's yard in North Holmwood and Arlington Cottage and his diggings had a huge impact on the landscape, North Holmwood pond probably having been formed when water from nearby springs filled his excavations. (Not that the business was successful: Miller surrendered the property to his mortgagee after a few years. A later tenant, Joseph Peters, went bankrupt in 1819 with stocks of 16,000 bricks, 200 pantiles, 110 sea kale pots, 20 chimneypots, 1020 drainpipes, and 350 greenhouse pots. By the 1830s the pottery was no longer operational.)

18th century Priory Cottage is one of a number that grew up around the Nag's Head with orchards behind it and the turnpike road in front.

In time the benefits of the road were mitigated by the effects of the agricultural revolution which resulted in increased productivity over much of the country, causing falls in grain prices nationwide. Low prices demanded increased productivity, but with their poor soils, limited crops and transport difficulties, Surrey farmers were at a disadvantage. Newly developed techniques and machinery were defeated by the intractable clay

Situated on the track from Betchets Green towards Anstie Cherry Tree Cottage was built in the mid-18th century. It has a 19th century bake-house attached.

and as the eighteenth century went on farm workers were increasingly in thrall to the vagaries of grain prices and low wages.

If farming was difficult, the isolated Holmwood was ideal for smuggling. In the late eighteenth and early nineteenth centuries prohibitive duties made lawful trade with continental Europe hardly worthwhile; demand was, therefore, satisfied by the illegal trade. Contraband goods were brought up from the Sussex coast through Surrey. Smugglers travelled by night and by isolated tracks through the sparsely populated Redlands woods or over the Common, no doubt aided by impoverished commoners. Tales abound: of skirmishes with customs men at Betchets Green, at the beershop, (reputedly known as the Bottle and Glass), on the Blackbrook road and at the Nag's Head, where those involved would allegedly refresh themselves before branching off onto the by-roads by which they avoided town. William Dudley of Coldharbour, who died in 1902, aged 101, recalled that a man with whom he worked had been a witness when the turnpike keeper refused to open his gate at night to brandy smugglers with kegs on their horses. John Tilt, who inhabited a string of properties on the fringes of the Common in the late eighteenth century - Redlands, Betchets Green and Anstie farms in the east and Heathfields in the west - may have made considerable money from the trade to judge by the amount that he left in his will in 1811. Certainly his properties were ideally placed for those avoiding the turnpike.

Evidence is scarce and hearsay unreliable: folklore says that Spook Hill was named by smugglers who wished it to be believed that there were spirits thereabouts so

South Lodge was built in about 1790 as an estate cottage to Subberies Farm. Absorbed into the Holmwood Park estate it was later Holmwood's first schoolhouse and home to its teachers, the Dolmans.

24

that they would not be disturbed, however the area is recorded as *Spookland* centuries earlier; nor did 'spook' have the meaning of 'ghost' in the eighteenth century.

Whatever the reality, the Holmwood had a reputation as a lawless place, the pickings of the road and its isolation attracting criminals. Stories abound of desperate squatters in the years of the Revolutionary and Napoleonic Wars when lack of imports forced grain prices high, and in the isolated lands west of the turnpike road, between Redlands and Coldharbour, was 'Robbing Gate', the name of which suggests the character of the district.

Such law and order as there was was kept by elected constables. In the event of crime advertisements would be printed offering rewards for information, the cost of which, together with that of any prosecution, would be borne by the victim. At the end of the eighteenth century Holmwood property owners joined together to maintain a kitty out of which such costs might be paid should any member fall victim to crime. The Beare Green Prosecuting Society met at the Duke's Head. Members ranged from the Duke through minor gentry, farmers and shopkeepers to innkeepers from Dorking to the Sussex borders. Rewards were payable for information in cases of murder, house-breaking, arson, highway robbery, theft, and the receiving of stolen goods. The Society's accounts mainly record the theft of livestock: geese, rabbits and the occasional horse.

Contributing to the lawlessness in later years were billeted soldiery for with the Revolutionary and Napoleonic Wars spanning a period of twenty-five years on and off at the turn of the century soldiers were commonly sent south towards the coast, often causing mayhem. In 1809 a party about to join the ill-fated Walcheren Expedition got so drunk at the Duke's Head that they fried their watches and ate banknote sandwiches.

Most of the crime had its roots in rural poverty, however, exacerbated during the war years as restricted imports kept corn prices high. Those with no land were dependent upon casual work and those who found no demand for their labours found themselves and their

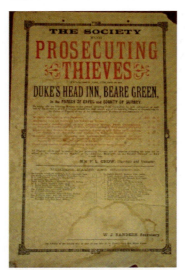

By the time of this poster the Beare Green Prosecuting Society was largely a social network though it paid out until 1912 for information leading to the apprehension of duck thieves, petty arsonists and the like. *(Dorking Museum)*

families, with the old and the sick, the responsibility of the Dorking parish overseers who ran a workhouse and attempted to get paupers into work. Holmwood's representatives as overseer reflect the diversity of businesses in the district: butchers, wheelwrights, blacksmiths, brickmakers, carpenters, brewers and millers. Their workhouse keeper utilised the labours of such paupers as were able to work, his capital and skill enabling the paupers to work for their livings to his profit. For this purpose Nathanial Wix, who occupied the position in Dorking from the 1760s to 1790s, purchased two cottages – Moor Cottage and Stoneheal - with rights of common in Holmwood.

Rights of common had become something of a battleground by the end of the century, however. Traditional abuses continued: in the 1780s Henry Swan's men dug and enclosed an illegal sawpit near the mill; in 1793 Gideon Longhurst and William Peters were using an illegally enclosed piece of the Common for lime burning and in all likelihood some of the wood necessary for individual farmers' temporary kilns which dotted the 'kiln' fields came illegally from the Common. The common driver's was not a pleasant job: in 1784 Ben Alloway was assaulted while going about the business of enforcement.

It was their commoners' rights that made agricultural work viable for many labourers and legitimate commoners met with the Lord's agent to agree policy on the use of the Common. At public meetings it would be agreed how much furze and fern might be cut and at what rate, whether and where brick kilns should be sited or clay dug or earth taken. With a growing population, however, conflict arose, not just between Lord and commoner, but between legitimate commoners and unauthorised users who sought to appropriate the Common's resources for by the early nineteenth century the Common was being illegally exploited on an industrial scale. Furze, wood, holly, turf, leaf mould, dung, brick earth and gravel were pillaged without consent; animals were run by those with no entitlement; sheds, lime kilns and wood houses were unlawfully situated and fences surreptitiously moved. In 1807 William Randall was fined for cutting ferns by the wagon-load and selling them out of the Manor, in effect, theft. Clay digging was so endemic that it was ordered in 1810 that there be no more brick earth digging nor carrying away of cattle dung on pain of a fine of forty shillings. Nonetheless the miller, William Bishop, was still removing it for his brick kilns and in 1817 James Peters illegally enclosed a brick yard and was digging earth for pottery leaving holes that were a danger to people and cattle.

In the years after 1815 when corn prices fell with the resumption of imports and with them wages access to the Common's resources might make the difference between survival and destitution. In October 1819, however, the Duke of Norfolk proposed enclosing the commons of the Manor of Dorking. Notices went out announcing his intention to petition Parliament so that the Common might be parcelled up and allotted to those who had rights over it in proportion to their holdings. Some thought that this would have a beneficial effect upon the thieves and idlers of the Holmwood, pointing out that the Holmwood was *the resort of vagabonds and poachers and notoriously a public nuisance'* from which idlers took dishonest livings. The existence of the Common, argued Thomas Hope of the Deepdene and his allies, far from fostering honest labour only encouraged dishonest practice, providing '*a harbour for thieves, vagabonds and idle and disorderly people of all kinds'*. Enclosing the Common and turning it to cultivation, he argued, would remove the opportunity for idling and create more legitimate work, so fostering honest industry. And more work would relieve local poverty – a considerable advantage to those who had to bear the costs of poor relief. However, those against argued that rather than relieving poverty, denial of the Common's resources to those who supplemented meagre or non existent labouring incomes would cause many more to fall into destitution, resulting in even higher poor rates.

At a public meeting held at the Red Lion in Dorking debate was fierce. What some with small pieces of land benefiting from common rights stood to gain was far outweighed by the loss of their grazing rights. Others who grazed little but who had substantial rights might rather have had a portion of land that they might farm or sell to developers. Mr Barclay of Bury Hill was not in favour nor Henry Peters of Betchworth Castle. Perhaps if the Duke had had pressing concerns in the area or if soils had been better, the slopes less steep and the ground less wet, making the profit argument more clear-cut, the proposition might have been carried. But though the Duke pushed through the enclosure of 720 acres in Horsham and the commoners of nearby Shellwood agreed to the enclosure of the small common there, the Holmwood remained unenclosed.

Generation Games - the Pledges and the Turners

Edward Pledge of the Sawyers' Arms was unable to sign his name when he contracted to buy wood from the Duke's copse at Hambrich. He was successful in business, however, and was followed as landlord by his son, Solomon, (who also started life as a wood worker), and granddaughter, Hannah.
The Turners of the White Hart were also several generations in the business.

Nonetheless the following years were hard ones in Holmwood. With prices low it was hard to make a profit on Holmwood's labour-intensive clays. Casual wages fell as farmers sought to compete as did the amount of land in cultivation as unprofitably labour-intensive areas were abandoned, diminishing the work available. Increasing numbers sought relief from their parishes throughout the 1820s and many Holmwood farmers were summonsed for non-payment of their poor rates. In 1820 the parish of Dorking proposed the building of houses on the Common for those unable to house themselves - the vestry already rented some cottages at Betchets Green for the purpose - and in 1821 and 1822 appeals were made to the Duke for enclosure of areas of the Common that might be cultivated in the hope of creating work. The Duke, however, was not in a position to give such consent.

Rural unrest all over Britain came to a head in 1830 when bad harvests pushed corn prices up. At Trouts Farm, bordering Moorhurst, and at Breakspeares, corn stacks were burned and it is likely that Holmwood labourers were amongst the desperate mob which descended on Dorking to protest at the inadequacy of local wages, the subsequent meeting - at the Red Lion - escalating into a riot. Shortly afterwards some of these desperate souls took the opportunity to emigrate to Canada under the Dorking emigration scheme, amongst them Charles Cosins who had occupied Redlands Farm, his wife and twelve children.

Bleak times indeed.

A 16th century smoke-bay house and a small chimney house both lurk within the 18th and 19th century additions to Moorhurst. The name comes from Moorers, as the farm was known in the 17th century when it was owned by the Constable family of Capel.

In the early 19th century the farm was acquired by the Duke of Norfolk, then sold to George Heath of Kitlands. The renovated farm house was later occupied by Heath's daughter, Julia, and son-in-law, James Park Harrison, then by his son Sir Leopold and, in the early 20th century, by Lord Ashbourne. It is sometimes known as Moorhurst Manor though there was never a manor of Moorhurst.

Quakers in the Holmwoods

The size of Wealden parishes and the remoteness of settlements favoured the growth of religious nonconformity in areas like Holmwood. The Bax family, who lived at Kitlands for at least 400 years, were amongst the first adherents to the Quaker faith, establishing a monthly meeting at the farm in 1655 when the movement was introduced into Surrey. Other adherents were the Peters family of Betchets Green and the Swan family of Bregsells.

In 1908 William Nash wrote a memoir of his time at Bregsells as a farm pupil lodging with Mr John Sargent, his wife and another pupil, Edward Trusted Bennett, all of whom were of the faith. They attended meetings in Capel, (where there was a community centred on Pleyestowe), rising every morning at five for lessons before breakfast at six-thirty. Isolated from their brethren, they would walk to meetings as far afield as Dorking, Reigate, Guildford or Horsham.

Fine houses for gentlemen

In 1649 the Duke of Norfolk's surveyor remarked upon the Manor's *pleasant hills and... salubrious air'*. Three years later Charles Howard, the Duke's son, built himself a house at 'Dibden', between Dorking and Holmwood, buying up neighbouring lands to create a small estate. By the 1740s word had spread. Emmanuel Bowen's map proclaimed the wholesome air of 'Darking', esteemed the sweetest in England, and over the course of the eighteenth century farms to the west, south and east of the town passed from the ownership of aristocratic or farmer landlords into the country estates of vastly wealthy London merchants and financiers.

To the west of the Common Edward Walter bought numerous farms to create the Bury Hill estate of 1600 acres in 1735. Virtually all the land bordering Holmwood on the west was subsumed into it, including Anstie, White House (Folly) and Redlands farms. After the death of Walter's son-in-law, Viscount Grimston, Robert Barclay, a wealthy Southwark brewer, purchased the mansion with its ornamental lakes and some of the estate in 1812[15].

In 1790 the Deepdene's Palladian mansion was sold to the heir to a banking fortune, Thomas Hope. And in 1798 Betchworth Castle and its thousand acres stretching from the zigzag at Box Hill to beyond Blackbrook passed from the Brownes to Henry Peters, a director of the Bank of England. It offered a country residence with hunting and riding within coaching distance of his place of work. The age of the city commuter had begun.

Coach travel was swifter, more comfortable, and less of an ordeal. By the 1820s the turnpike was carrying sixteen coaches a day through Holmwood. The mail left Horsham at ten at night for London, being returned at seven in the morning. The Horsham 'Star' travelled the thirty-eight miles to London in three and a half hours, changing horses at the Duke's Head then at Dorking, Leatherhead and three further stops. Horsham to Dorking coaches were slower, but the Arundel 'Comet', the Worthing, Bognor and Littlehampton 'Accommodation', and the Brighton 'Sovereign' and 'William IV' all called daily. By mid-century the

James Edwards' map, surveyed in 1787, shows the small residential enclosures out of the Common that would be gentrified and upgraded in the coming century.

---

[15] The Duke of Norfolk picked up some farms on the sales of the Bury Hill and Betchworth Castle estates.

Holmwood toll-gate was taking two hundred and fifty pounds a year.

In the 1820s the turnpike was re-routed at North Holmwood, abandoning the steep climb over the Common to pass Spookland at a lower level. Much of the diggings from the pottery were infilled at this time, leaving a small pond. As a result of the diversion, the Nag's Head found itself no longer at the roadside. The Norfolk Arms was built opposite a few years later. Though another of the Turner family took the tenancy, unlike the White Hart and the Sawyers', the Norfolk was no local venture: it was owned by Heathfield Young, whose Dorking-based brewing family owned scores of inns.

There was nothing in or about the Common that could be described as a village at the beginning of the nineteenth century, however. But changes were afoot: improvements in the comfort and speed of travel meant that the hills south of Dorking were now accessible not just to the exceedingly wealthy whose money could insulate them from the inconveniences of life in the countryside, but to those with the leisure to drive out, both from the town and from further afield. Pigot's 1823 'London Directory' claimed views equal to the finest in Italy for Dorking. John Timbs' 'Picturesque Promenade Round Dorking' recommended Holmwood's hills, dales, and orchards. The increasing availability of carriage travel saw more modest professionals building their mansions in Dorking or on the approaches to it and soon the wild and lawless communities of the Holmwood came to the attention of such seekers after tranquillity.

In 1823 the Bax family sold Kitlands Farm between Coldharbour and South Holmwood to a London lawyer, George Heath. At Kitlands Heath created a substantial home to which he constructed a road from the turnpike. He then bought up neighbouring Trouts, Moorhurst and Anstie farms. With their vast family enclave the Heaths became the aristocracy of Holmwood.

In the same year auction particulars proclaimed Stumbleholt Farm *'easily convertible to a comfortable residence for a family or a gentleman fond of field sports.'*

Three years later Wymbletons Farm, just off the Common on the Betchworth side of the Newdigate road, was bought by a wealthy London 'dancing master', George Gough. It was neither the Heaths nor Gough who created the infrastructure of a village in the Holmwood, however, but another London-based family, the Larpents of Holmwood House.

Mrs Larpent, (born Charlotte Rosamund Arnold), had family connections with Holmwood. With her sister, Caroline, she had owned

Holmwood's early 19th century Independent Chapel. Now a dwelling, it was replaced by the new Baptist Chapel in 1874. Situated next to the Sundial it served as a tearoom known as the Well in the early 20th century and until the 1970s the front room and a stall in the garden served as Dawes' grocery.

Subberies Farm before her marriage and after it she and her husband acquired the adjacent Swites, together with smaller plots, to create an estate of 130 acres. At Subberies the Larpents built a Jacobean-style mansion named Holmwood House with two carriage drives, numerous cottages and three lodges, (one the refashioned Cinders Cottage, another the agricultural dwelling that became South Lodge.) Swites became the estate farm. Across the park, Holmwood Cottage was built for Mrs Larpent's mother, Mary Ann Arnold - though with a billiard room and 10 bedrooms it was pushing the definition of a cottage somewhat.

When these genteel pioneers arrived there was no church and no school in Holmwood. Religious needs were served by the Surrey Mission Society Chapel and the Holmwood Independent Chapel. The new gentry, however, had need of something more. At Mrs Larpent's instigation, therefore, the Duke of Norfolk made land available to the west of the turnpike directly opposite Holmwood House's carriage drive. Her mother provided an annuity for a new church and petitioned the Bishop of Winchester, claiming that more than three hundred people within the parishes of Dorking and Capel lived two miles or more from those churches. The population of the Holmwood, she claimed, was over seven hundred.

George Heath and Kitlands

George Heath was the son of James Heath, the celebrated engraver. His half-brothers engraved the penny black and his wife, Ann Raymond, was a descendent of John Napier, the inventor of logarithms; Sir John Moore of Corunna was her cousin. Ambivalent about her husband's foray into the Holmwood, she was compensated for the solitude and discomfort of Kitlands with a mansion at Marble Arch.

The renovated Kitlands as drawn by Heath's eldest daughter Julia. *(JJ Heath Caldwell)*

The Larpents of Holmwood House

Francis Seymour Larpent and his wife, Charlotte, arrived in Holmwood in 1830. Like George Heath he had made his money as a lawyer, twice being called upon to investigate the alleged sexual improprieties of Princess Caroline and to advise the Prince Regent on his divorce. He had also been Judge-Advocate to the forces under Wellington in the Peninsular War where he reformed the court martial system and was briefly taken prisoner by the French. His account of those times: 'The Private Journal of Judge Advocate Larpent' is still in print.

The Larpents retained a London residence as Mr Larpent continued to work as Chairman of the Audit Commissioners but so much had the quality of the roads improved by the 1830s that he was able to go frequently to London by coach, making him probably the first Holmwood commuter.

On her husband's death in 1845 Charlotte Larpent moved to Devon. She maintained contact with Holmwood all her life, however, leaving money to the school in her will. Holmwood House was inherited by her husband's half-brother, Baron John James de Hochpied Larpent, whose Hungarian title was inherited from his mother. *(National Portrait Gallery)*

Renamed Holmwood Park by a subsequent owner, the house was struck by an incendiary during the Second World War. Only a fragment remains. *Painting by ET Wickham. (Reproduced by permission of Surrey History Centre)*

Designed by John Burges Watson, (who designed Duck Island Cottage in St James' Park), St Mary Magdalene was small, simple and rustic with neither spire nor tower. Seating 275, (90 in the gallery), with two thirds of the seats reserved, it was consecrated in June 1838. A modest vicarage (Foxmead) by the same architect was built for the Reverend John Sutton Utterton a year later.

The boundaries of the new district of Holmwood ran from Rosewood Cottage, (known as Carpenter's cottage), down the turnpike to turn east at the Black Brook. It then ran south along the Blackbrook road to Ashbrook from whence it turned west to meet the turnpike again north of Beare Green then continuing west between Moorhurst and Arnolds farms to the junction of the Broome Hall and Kitlands estates, proceeding back north through Meridons Farm, (therefore covering much of Coldharbour), and Redlands.

St Mary Magdalene, South Holmwood

St Mary Magdalene in a drawing dedicated to Mrs Arnold by John Burges Watson. The addition of a chancel, a north extension with tower, a vestry and a south extension with a porch have made it almost unrecognisable. In the background can be seen the farm known as Cowpers, part of which formed Nettlefold's pits. In the 1880s the farm was sold for housing, forming Norfolk, Buckingham and Warwick Roads, with Church Terrace built on the site of the farmhouse.
(Reproduced by permission of Surrey History Centre)

The memorial window to Mary Ann Arnold is tucked away in the tower at St Mary Magdalene. It depicts the construction of the tiny church in 1838 though the labourers appear to be wearing medieval dress. An adjacent window depicts the Good Samaritan bringing the traveller in need to the door of St Mary Magdalene, an apt image for a roadside chapel as it then was.

When Holmwood's first incumbent, the young Reverend Utterton, arrived in Holmwood to take up his appointment he was told that Julia Heath had sold some jewellery and Charlotte Larpent some paintings in order to fund the building of the church. He described his living as 'a paradise'.

It was only a matter of years, however, before the congregation had outgrown the modest chapel and the 19th century saw extension after extension as the population of Holmwood grew.

Mrs Larpent then turned her attention to education, engaging John Dolman to teach local boys at a hut beside Moor Cottage; his wife, Elizabeth, took the girls at South Lodge. In 1844 a schoolhouse with master's lodging was commissioned. It was built half a mile south of the church – again on land donated by the Duke. Schooling, of course, was not compulsory and many were unable to spare their children from their labours whilst the studies of those who did attend were interrupted for sowing, bird-scaring and harvesting.

Four years later Mrs Larpent and the Rev Utterton were granted another plot where the turnpike met the Betchets Green track. Nothing came of their plan to build almshouses, however, perhaps because Mrs Larpent moved on after the death of her husband.

Julia Heath and South Holmwood School

The school was designed by James Park Harrison, husband of Julia, elder daughter of George Heath. (Her brother, Douglas Denon, was a trustee.) He had previously designed St John the Evangelist in Redhill and Holy Trinity, Rudgwick, whilst Julia was one of the first to comment to Tennyson on his 'In Memoriam' when parts of it were sent to her brothers, Douglas Denon and John Moore, before publication. The couple lived for some time at Moorhurst. *(JJ Heath Caldwell/School photograph reproduced by permission of Surrey History Centre)*

By the 1840s the most densely settled area of the Common was that around the Old Nag's and the Norfolk with its stables, cottages and orchards opposite which stood the animal pound. More cottages with orchards and gardens hugged the roadside there; others nestled down the lane that lead towards Inholms and the Black Brook, the labourers' dwellings of Laurel, Daisy and Ivy Porch cottages sandwiched between farm and Common, Littlebrook and Brookmeadow farms hugging the stream. Further north were the 'potteries' of North Holmwood and the scattered cottages of Spook Hill with orchards running along the western side of the road from whence a string of cottages now ran from Rosewood Cottage past Redlands Farm to the mill.

The occupants of these cottages remained rural in occupation, labourers, lath cleaners, lime burners, hoop shavers and basket makers. Most had been born locally, or no further away than Newdigate, Rusper or Capel. For them poverty still prevailed and from 1836, when the Dorking Union was formed, outside aid could no longer be expected. Should they be unable to work, whether through age, accident or infection, (as during the Holmwood cholera outbreak of 1842), they and their families were admitted to the Dorking workhouse.

Nor was the area more law-abiding. When Dorking's first police officer was appointed in 1838 the theft of a colt from Holmwood was amongst his early cases. Another concerned the discovery at the Holmwood house of one James Gibbs of thirteen stolen chickens: the miscreant was taken into custody from the Norfolk. Livestock remained at risk on the Common: 'hue and cry' ensued in 1841 after the loss of a horse from Breakspeares; an offender was sentenced to six months hard labour in 1845 for the theft of geese belonging to Joseph Turner of the White Hart; handbills were printed on the theft of rabbits in 1853; in 1860 William Wood of Beare Green was unable to recover a stolen horse and in 1868 James Rose of Goldenlands, near Stonebridge, was allowed expenses by the Prosecuting Society in an attempt to apprehend night thieves who had taken a horse and cash.

Before the 1850s were out there was another attempt to enclose this den of 'thieves and vagabonds'. Signatures to the petition against, lead by Mrs Larpent, Mrs Arnold, George Gough and the Rev Utterton, ran into hundreds. Though they made much of the interests of the poor, it cannot have escaped their notice that the Common subsidised a labour source and that an enclosed common was unlikely to be farmed but rather sold piecemeal for housing.

For the Holmwood was becoming known. In 1854 Holmwood House featured in Burke's 'Visitation of the Seats and Arms of the Noblemen and Gentlemen of Great Britain'. By 1855 its reputation was made. It was *a favourite resort of individuals desirous of enjoying the most salubrious air and delightful scenery*, claimed the auctioneers when the mill came onto the market, reporting a *rapid increase of population in the immediate neighbourhood, both as regards numbers and respectability*.

The 1840s had seen George Rennie, the civil engineer and bridge designer, building a mansion on a squatter's enclosure by Stubs Farm. The 1850s saw a building boom. Ancient dwellings demolished, given brick skins and hung with tiles or refashioned into parts of much grander ones. Lady MacDonald of Amersham built the Knoll in 1854. Brook Lodge, (on the site of the beerhouse on the Blackbrook road), went up the following year, followed by Oakdale, (on the site of a cluster of cottages, orchards and brick workings), in 1865 and Eutrie House in 1866 – all of them close to Holmwood House and the church.

George Rennie and Holmwood Lodge

The son of the great bridge designer, John, George Rennie assisted in the design and construction of Waterloo Bridge, did the calculations for the arches at Southwark Bridge and claimed the design of London Bridge (now in Lake Havasu City, Arizona). Though he also practised as a railway engineer, (and probably came across Holmwood when he and his brother surveyed the line for a proposed route from London to Brighton with a branch to Dorking in the 1830s), he is best known for his mechanical genius, in particular for the naval work carried out by J&G Rennie at Greenwich which supplied steamship engines, including that for the 'Dwarf', the first screw-propelled vessel to be operated by the British Navy. He is buried in South Holmwood where his memorial depicts the three arches of Southwark Bridge. Holmwood Lodge stood opposite the site that became North Holmwood church, now Lodge Close, North Close, the Orchard and St Johns. *Painting by John Linnel (National Portrait Gallery); Photograph Dorking Museum*

Tennyson and the Heath Brothers

 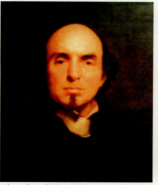 

Douglas Denon Heath (left) and his brother John Moore (middle) were close friends of Tennyson at Cambridge and members of the Apostles group with Arthur Hallam. Tennyson visited Kitlands in 1834 and John Moore became engaged to his sister, Mary, though the marriage never took place, causing a rift between the families.

Their father, George, employed the botanist, Sir William Hooker, and his specimen collecting son Sir Joseph Dalton Hooker, (both later directors at Kew Gardens), in the creation of his gardens at Kitlands. The Himalayan Rhododendron Falconeri (above) was drawn by the celebrated botanical artist, Marianne North, whose work is on permanent display at Kew, at Kitlands.

On George Heath's death in 1852 Douglas Denon, (like his father a lawyer, but a private man of scholarly interests), inherited Kitlands. *(Photograph Dorking Museum; painting by permission of JJ Heath Caldwell; drawing by permission of the Trustees of the Royal Botanic Gardens, Kew)*

In 1856 a service was held at St Mary Magdalene to celebrate the return of Douglas Denon's younger brother, Captain Leopold, from the Crimea where he had been commander of transport at Balaclava. He took up residence at Moorhurst, now refashioned into a gentleman's residence. In 1868 Leopold received a knighthood after commanding the expedition to rescue the British Consul imprisoned by the King of Abyssinia. He was later promoted to Admiral. With his wife, Mary Ann Marsh, Sir Leopold built a grand new residence, the 26-bedroomed Anstie Grange, in the 1860s. The three family residences – Anstie, Moorhurst and Kitlands - with their farms and cottages comprised over six hundred and fifty acres. Rising to over a thousand acres during the stewardship of Leopold's son, Cuthbert, the estates housed the extended family for generations. *(JJ Heath Caldwell)*

With the building boom came work, for locals and for incomers, alleviating the effects of agricultural poverty. James Croucher had established a brickyard at Stubs Farm by 1860 and local men set up as bricklayers whilst women undertook dressmaking and laundry. Pedlars and brush makers appeared whilst gypsies are recalled in the name Little Egypt – later Egypt Cottages – where Sefton Villas now stand in North Holmwood. The grand houses created a market for tradesmen of all sorts: with just one bakery and a couple of butchers in Holmwood in 1841, by 1851 there was a general store and four grocers. Five years later there were tailors, a bootmaker, a potter, carpenters, brick and tile merchants and a post office just off the turnpike on what would become Warwick Road. With proximity to the mansions, development at 'South Holmwood' – between Folly

George Gough's late Georgian residence at Wymbletons was built in much the same style as the contemporaneous Norfolk Arms, in all probability on the site of an older farmhouse. Neighbouring Kiln (Holly) Cottage and Four Wents Cottage were all part of the farm and Gough also tenanted the adjacent Posterns Farm. In use since at least the 1640s, the name probably comes from the Wymmylton family who were farming at Stubs in the 1580s.

Farm and Betchets Green - now eclipsed the area around the Norfolk.

Land within the Holmwood became valuable. As early as 1857 Baron de Hochpied Larpent - resident in Brussels – who had just built Grandon Lodge as a dower house, proposed forming a company to construct modest villas on his estate - only twenty-five years after its creation. He died, however, in 1860, before anything came of his plan.

Not surprisingly, just a few years after it was built, St Mary Magdalene was found to have insufficient capacity. In 1842 a chancel designed by James William Wild added 150 seats. A north aisle with tower was added in 1845 to commemorate the marriage of George Heath's second daughter, Emma Jane, to the banker William Godfrey Whatman. To the west Coldharbour was also growing and in 1848 the boundaries of Dorking, Holmwood, Capel, Wotton and Ockley were re-worked on John Labouchere's endowment of a church there. A chunk of Holmwood district was removed to form part of the new district of Coldharbour. It was replaced with a swathe in the north stretching as far as the potteries. It therefore became necessary to provide for the education of the children in that area who were no longer the responsibility of Dorking district. A separate infant school was established there in 1849. Older

St Mary Magdalene with Wild's chancel extension of 1842. It was probably built in commemoration of the marriage of Julia Heath to the architect James Park Harrison. *(Reproduced by permission of Surrey History Centre)*

children had to walk to Mrs Larpent's school.

By the time of the religious census of 1851, (and before the great building boom), three hundred and fifty people were attending morning service, with four hundred in the afternoon and over a hundred children present at Sunday school morning and afternoon[16]. This was in addition to the score attending the Surrey Mission Society Chapel and the fifty at the Holmwood Independent Chapel. By 1853 even the burial ground was inadequate and the Duke had to make another grant of land next to Vigo to be used as a kitchen garden so that a part of the vicarage's kitchen garden might be given up to the burial ground.

By the later nineteenth century even the nature of local farms had changed. Many had become 'estate' farms[17]: Kitlands, Moorhurst Anstie, Trouts, Swites and Subberies were owned by the lawyers, Heath and Larpent, Stubs and Inholms by the Hope family of bankers at the Deepdene, Wymbletons by Gough, the dancing master, Spookland by Charles Barclay of Bury Hill, whose fortune derived from brewing, whilst Vigo and Breakspeares were part of Henry Lazenby's three hundred or more acres (and would soon enough be swallowed into the Oakdene estate). John Gilliam Stilwell, who bought Bregsells in 1852, had made his money at the Stilwell Bank in London (though his family originated in Dorking). These 'pleasure farms' were not their owners' main source of income, nor, with their lawns and shrubberies, did they provide a great deal of labouring work.

The farms may have been largely subsumed but scores of independent holdings remained. Some ran to five or ten acres or more; others had been broken down into innumerable plots housing labourers' and tradesmen's cottages with gardens or a small orchard. By the 1860s the Holmwood was only semi-agricultural, with many making a living in trade or at the big houses, but the Common still played a large part in the economic life of many of those who lived in and around it. Many grazed geese, ducks or pigs or gathered acorns or berries or bracken which provided animal bedding in winter that manured the land in the spring. In August notices would announce the date the bracken might be claimed, on which day those with rights of common would assemble early to cut around the patch that they wished to claim. Harvesting could then be carried out later. It was a procedure that went

The north aisle and tower were added to St Mary Magdalene in commemoration of the marriage of George Heath's younger daughter, Emma Jane, to the banker William Godfrey Whatman in 1848. The painting, as several others in this book, is by Emmeline Wickham, eldest daughter of the Rev Wickham. Emmeline married the scholar James Clark Bright who became master of University College, Oxford. When she died at 33 leaving four children under five her sister Julia went to live with her widower as housekeeper. *(Reproduced by permission of Surrey History Centre)*

---

[16] A curate, William James Collin, had been taken on by this time.

[17] The exceptions were Redlands, Bentsbrook and Protridges which were in the hands of the Steeres

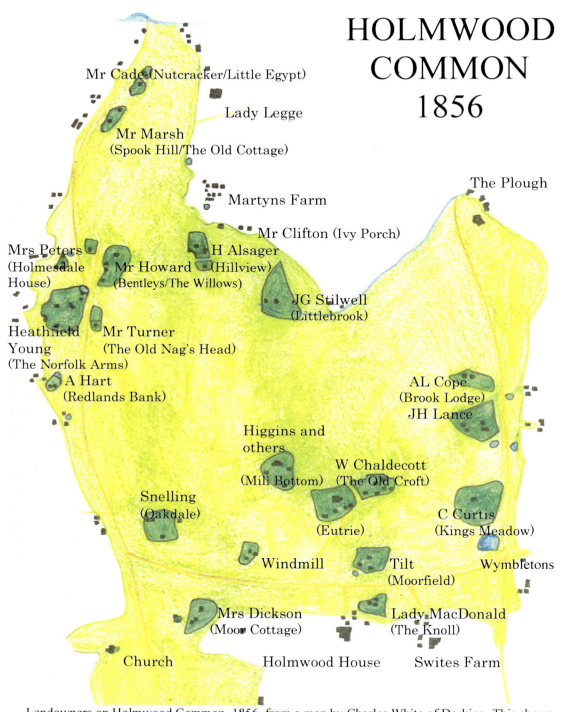

HOLMWOOD COMMON 1856

Mr Cade (Nutcracker/Little Egypt)

Lady Legge

Mr Marsh
(Spook Hill/The Old Cottage)

The Plough

Martyns Farm

Mr Clifton (Ivy Porch)

Mrs Peters
(Holmesdale
House)

H Alsager
(Hillview)

Mr Howard
(Bentleys/The Willows)

JG Stilwell
(Littlebrook)

Heathfield
Young
(The Norfolk Arms)

Mr Turner
(The Old Nag's Head)

AL Cope
(Brook Lodge)
JH Lance

A Hart
(Redlands Bank)

Higgins and
others

(Mill Bottom)

W Chaldecott
(The Old Croft)

Snelling
(Oakdale)

C Curtis
(Kings Meadow)

(Eutrie)

Windmill

Tilt
(Moorfield)

Wymbletons

Mrs Dickson
(Moor Cottage)

Lady MacDonald
(The Knoll)

Church

Holmwood House

Swites Farm

Landowners on Holmwood Common, 1856, from a map by Charles White of Dorking. This shows
the period of transition from lowly agricultural dwellings to grand houses. One or two wealthy
profesionals are in residence – Mr Lance at Brook Lodge, the widowed Lady Anne MacDonald at
the Knoll – but most of the dwellings are still owned by local landowners – the Tilts and Stilwells,
Drs Curtis and Chaldecott of Dorking, Heathfield Young, the loal brewer – and tenanted.

on into the twentieth century in Holmwood.

In 1858 the 'Illustrated Handbook of Dorking' described Holmwood Common as *'covered with bushes and furze, its rough, short grass trimmed by horses and cattle, with cottages and several grand mansions scattered about'*. It was also home to numerous lodging houses. No longer a place to be avoided, so many households were making a supplementary income from summer visitors that there were

Bregsells farm was recorded in the 13th century in the ownership of the de Brugeshulle family. By the 19th it was owned by John Gilliam Stilwell, whose father, Thomas - his wife's family owned Littlebrook Farm in the middle of the Common - had found fortune in London, rising from clerk to partner in the naval agency, Sykes and Son. A friend of the polar explorer, Captain John Ross, and of Lord Byron, he saw the firm's transition into the Stilwell banking house in which his son became a partner. The family later added Betchets Green Cottage and Folly Farm to its portfolio. Bregsells burned down in 1913. *(Surrey Archaeological Society)*

concerns about the Common's preservation. Hence a committee – with Baron de Hochpied in the chair - was formed to act in partnership with the Duke in its protection. Its first act was to appoint a ranger, William Lipscombe, to prevent the taking of wood and holly by those with no entitlement.

The formation of a committee was typical of Holmwood's new social and benevolent aristocracy; by mid-century the newly arrived great and good, in partnership with the church, were taking responsibility for the care of the poor, the old and the sick, for social welfare, education and road maintenance. Often taking the lead in such matters was the Reverend Wickham who sat on scores of committees over the fifty years of his ministry. In the early 1860s it was a committee which raised the money for a south aisle at St Mary Magdalene and the same wealthy coterie took responsibility for the operation of the turnpike, the term of which was extended for a third time in 1858 when the trustees included the Barclays, the Hopes, de Hochpied, Wickham, John Gilliam Stilwell and Edward Swan's executors.

The parish was still burdened with general road maintenance, however. In 1857 it undertook improvements at North Holmwood, where, since the diversion of the turnpike twenty-five years earlier, Inholms Lane had been left short of a connection with it. A lane was no doubt already in practical use but it was equally certainly little more than a bog.

By late mid-century South Holmwood was thriving. It was hardly a community, however. The grand houses were secluded from the road and spaced at a discreet distance from one another. These were houses that proclaimed their affluence, that could import whatever and whoever they needed. They had little relationship with the clusters of dwellings and businesses at 'the potteries', at the Norfolk and at the Old Nag's Head which had grown up according to the dictates of the road. Nor had the coming of the wealthy changed the character of those areas overnight: on April 25th 1840 Dorking's police constable reports that: '*In the evening I went to the Holmwood with Mr Charles Alloway and apprehended James Sayer for being drunk and fighting with William Lucas who died on the spot where they had been fighting.*' Sayer was remanded the next day and on the 28th he was committed for trial for manslaughter. It was not an isolated incidence of crime in connection with drink: Constable Donaldson's occurrence book records disturbances caused by soldiers quartered at the Norfolk who threatened to burn the place down and the incarceration of one George Turley on a charge of robbery at the inn.

The coming of the grand houses would take some while to gentrify the roadside taverns of the Holmwood and the Norfolk Arms would retain its reputation for having a clientele of 'suspect persons' until very late in the century.

Reverend Edmund Dawe Wickham

The Rev Edmund Dawe Wickham, his family and the extended vicarage. Wickham arrived in Holmwood in 1851 and stayed half a century. A wealthy man who invested in a large amount of land locally, he and his wife, Emma, had 8 children. He moved in intellectual circles; his sons played cricket for Oxford and Somerset whilst his daughters married influential scholars. The Wickhams lived in style, extending the modest vicarage into a grand residence: in 1871 it was home to a German governess, a nurse a, cook, three maids and a page. Later a butler was employed and a cottage built for the gardener.

The frontispiece painting to this book, of St Mary Magdalene with its 1862 south aisle extension seen from Betchets Green Farm, is another by Wickham's daughter, Emmeline. The south aisle was designed by a Mr St Aubyn, probably James St Aubyn, the architect responsible for the restoration of St Michael's Mount. In the mid 19th century the church and vicarage were surrounded by thatched buildings. *(Reproduced by permission of Surrey History Centre)*

The two Olympias – St Mary Magdalene's Cazalet memorials

1848 saw the installation of two of St Mary Magdalene's most impressive memorials. The first, a window in the tower, commemorates the lives of Olympia Cazalet and her infant daughter, Frances. Born into the wealthy Anglo-Russian Cazalet family, (which had branched from trade into banking), Olympia had married her cousin, Peter Clement Cazalet to whom there was once also a memorial window at St Mary Magdalene. He divided his time between homes in London, St Petersburg, Brighton and Holmwood; the couple's son, William Clement, later put together an estate of 1000 acres at Grenehurst in Capel where he lived with his wife and seven daughters. Various members of the Cazalet family spent time in Holmwood, at the Knoll and Holmwood Cottage.

The second memorial is the magnificent relief on the south aisle which was raised by the husband of Olympia Henderson, depicting her grave in Lausanne where she died aged 31 with her baby daughter, also Olympia. Also born a Cazalet - the name Olympia runs through the family – Olympia Henderson was a grand-daughter of Mrs Arnold and closely related to Peter Clement and Olympia..

The coming of the railway

The London to Brighton & South Coast Railway named locomotives after villages and beauty spots on its routes – Deepdene, Denbies, Dorking and Boxhill.

From Dorking the railway line headed out towards Betchworth rather than directly south to avoid the steep rises towards Leith Hill. It still had to negotiate a climb of 350 feet, however, and the curve east of Holmwood lengthened the climb, so easing the gradient with the result that the station had to be situated south of the village on a bridge which carried the turnpike over the line. Even so, the pull up to Holmwood was always difficult under steam.
(Dorking Museum)

In 1867 the railway came to Holmwood. Promoted by the Horsham, Dorking & Leatherhead Railway at the instigation of local landowners, (primarily John Labouchere of Broome Hall), the line south from Leatherhead was completed by the London to Brighton & South Coast Railway. From Dorking it passed east towards Betchworth, curving west past Wymbletons and across Bregsells towards Horsham. Dorking station opened in March 1867. Construction problems on the Betchworth Tunnel delayed the Holmwood section until the first of May.

Signposted 'Holmwood for Leith Hill', the station was situated on a bridge over the track where the line passed under the Horsham road. It housed a ladies' room, a parcels' and left-luggage office, waiting room and booking office and a few yards to the south stood the Georgian-style station master's house. There were shelters on each platform and a footbridge with a glazed roof connected the two. Passenger services ran between London Bridge and Brighton via Horsham but there were also extensive goods yards and animal pens.

The villages might now be reached from London in little over an hour. Leith Hill became a day excursion. Leisure guides described walks from the station, copies of which, with fares advertised in the back, were kept in public reading rooms in the London suburbs. Holmwood was *'thick with gorse, bracken and low trees – undulating, beautiful, most picturesque'*, reported Japp's in 1881, before recommending a walk from Coldharbour through Kitlands and Moorhurst towards the station, past the *'very superior'* schoolhouse and the rectory, *'embowered in roses'*. Holmwood was a destination.

Some came for the day; others stayed. Even before the coming of the line directories like the 'Companionable Guide to Dorking' were commending the Common and its lodging houses. Visitors, they said, found *'health and pleasure in rusticating on [the] waste'* which was *'alive with geese and children'*. Cottages were advertised in the Dorking directories, larger properties in The Times, and families would take them for weeks or even months at a time, hiring staff for their stay.

Holmwood's tourist trade

The landlords of the old coaching inns found new business for their stables in the summer visitors: Charles Taylor, landlord at the Norfolk in the 1880s, like Daniel Fairbrother of the Windmill on Flint Hill, let carriages, wagonettes and pony chaises to those wanting to go out onto the hills. *(Dorking Museum)*

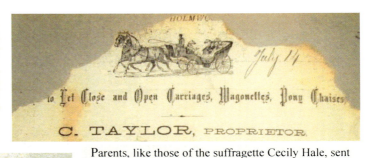

Parents, like those of the suffragette Cecily Hale, sent their children down with nannies, joining them when commitments allowed. Occupying the Hermitage at South Holmwood one year and Tollgate Cottage another, the Hale family were typical in employing a gardener and cleaner and having their meat delivered, with milk arriving in pails from a yoke across the shoulders of a local girl. For picnicking expeditions to Friday Street, Redlands, Coldharbour and Leith Hill they hired horse-drawn vehicles.

In 1858 – well before the coming of the railway to Holmwood – Sarah Clifton, wife of local butcher, Henry, was advertising furnished apartments at Ivy Porch Cottage, (the White Barn on Mid Holmwood Lane), accessed by coach or via the station in Dorking. The Cliftons and their descendents, the Knights, ran a lodging house there into the 20th century.
(Dorking Museum)

Coal, newspapers, telegrams: all came in via the station for distribution not just to the Holmwood residences but out to Coldharbour, Capel and Newdigate. To cater to the new trade Jack Buckland of Betchets Green carried luggage to and from the station, whilst John William Hoad, from Steyning on the old coach route, set up a horse-taxi business. At first confined to waiting at the station for trade, Hoad branched out into the carrying business, transporting luggage and parcels up to London, collecting goods from shops along the way and transporting them out to the villages. Soon he was offering a twice weekly service and by 1879 he had bought some land on the Horsham road on which he built his stables and a substantial house with outbuildings. This he named Steyning Cottage.

Even the hunt came in by train. The Surrey Union regularly hunted over the Common and adjoining farmland, keeping foxes down over a wide area. Hounds were centrally kept by the master of the hunt and many of Holmwood's great families participated in this expensive activity which had the support of locals who might otherwise lose livestock to the fox. Special trains ferried horses and hounds down to Holmwood for meets at Holmwood station, at Broome Hall or at Blackbrook.

The railways brought a great influx. Building materials could now be brought in by rail, being carried the last few miles by horse and cart. Coal for heating could be supplied and businesses in London were now within easy reach. Woodlands were shaped, views engineered, exotic trees planted and farms became 'pleasure farms' with specimen animals. Any land coming onto the market with the potential to form a country estate was advertised accordingly. If the hedges at Rushets near Stonebridge with its sixteen acres and brick kiln were grubbed, and the oaks put into groups, a park-like appearance might be achieved, suggested a selling agent in 1875. Then the land would be suitable for the erection of a 'gentleman's residence'.

Mansions of the railway age

Labouchere's widow, Mary Louisa, was one of the first to take advantage of the possibilities brought by the railway when she acquired part of Vigo Farm from the Reverend Wickham and created Oakdene (later renamed Capel Lyse).

The estate was enlarged by George Charles Spencer Churchill, Marquis of Blandford (brother of Winston Churchill's father, Randolph, and later 8th Duke of Marlborough). He added to it the rest of Vigo, the adjoining Breakspeares, (straddling the road), and Turners. The Marquis left somewhat ignominiously in 1876 after an affair with Lady Aylesford, leaving his wife and children in occupation. The estate was sold in 1881. After a spell in the ownership of the hop dealer, Wildman Cattley, it was bought in 1887 by Augustus Perkins of the Barclay and Perkins brewery. The area was a popular one with London brewers: the Barclays of Bury Hill had made their money in brewing, as had the Charringtons of Stumbleholt and the Farnell Watsons of Henfold to the south whilst part of Oakdene was later bought by Bertram Watney. *(Surrey Archaeological Society)*

Redlands was built in 1870 by the schools' architect Major Rohde Hawkins who trained with Thomas Cubitt (of Denbies) and designed North Holmwood church as well as a wing of Guy's Hospital. 'Major' was not a military title but his given name and 'Rohde' a family surname. With the seventy acre Redlands sandwiched between Oakdene's acres and the Heath estates of Kitlands, Moorhurst and Anstie, the whole of the south-western boundary of the Common was given over to stately residences, their farms and grounds. Redlands later became part of that Heath enclave when, towards the end of the century, it was occupied by Colonel Henry H Helsham Jones, his wife, Mary, and his sister, Henrietta, his daughter, Constance - by his first wife - being married to Sir Leopold's son, Frederick Crofton Heath Caldwell. (The Colonel's wife was related to Rohde Hawkins' wife, Mary Littledale Greenwood.) Between the houses there were shooting parties and dances.

To the south-east Oakdene adjoined Holmwood House, which, after the death of de Hochpied in 1860 lay empty whilst tenants were sought of *'known respectability without small children'*. In 1866 it was bought by John Gough Nichols, the antiquarian editor and publisher of the 'Gentleman's Magazine', and renamed Holmwood Park. Henfold and Wigmore lay adjacent to the south, all of them between a hundred and two hundred acres. *(Dorking Museum)*

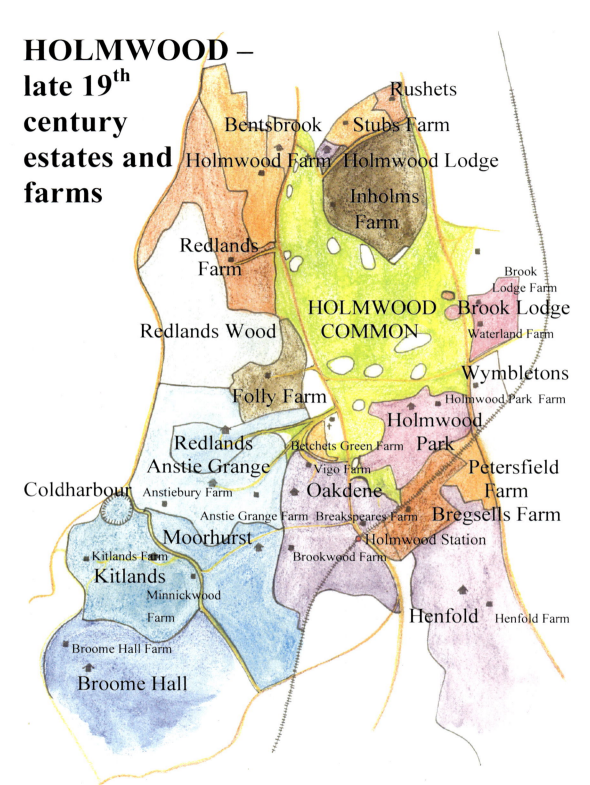

HOLMWOOD –
late 19th century estates and farms

Rushets

Bentsbrook   Stubs Farm

Holmwood Farm   Holmwood Lodge

Inholms Farm

Redlands Farm

Brook Lodge Farm

HOLMWOOD COMMON   Brook Lodge

Redlands Wood   Waterland Farm

Wymbletons

Folly Farm   Holmwood Park Farm

Holmwood

Redlands   Betchets Green Farm   Park

Anstie Grange   Vigo Farm   Petersfield Farm

Coldharbour   Anstiebury Farm   Oakdene

Bregsells Farm

Anstie Grange Farm   Breakspeares Farm

Moorhurst   Holmwood Station

Kitlands Farm   Brookwood Farm

Kitlands

Minnickwood Farm   Henfold   Henfold Farm

Broome Hall Farm

Broome Hall

The great estates surrounding the Holmwood with their farms. Independent farms are shown in brown. (Boundaries are approximate.)

Heaths and Helsham Jones

Colonel Henry H Helsham Jones, his daughter Constance, and her husband, Major General Frederick Crofton Heath Caldwell whom she had met when her father was stationed at Aldershot. (Sir Leopold's second son, he took the name Caldwell on receipt of an inheritance from his mother's family). The Colonel lived first at Vigo then Redlands, moving to Moorfield on the death of his wife, Mary. *(JJ Heath Caldwell)*

In 1870 the historian Henry Elliot Malden married Margaret Whatman, daughter of William Godfrey Whatman and his wife Emma Jane and grand-daughter of George Heath. He lived at Kitlands with a large family for the next sixteen years. *(Dorking Advertiser)*

All over Holmwood rough dwellings set in a few acres of land were replaced with substantial residences: Furzelea (later Moorfield) was built in 1868 on the site of a cluster of old cottages; Moor Lodge replaced Moor Cottage in 1875, like many others upgrading its designation from 'cottage to the more imposing 'lodge'. On the eastern edge of the Common Posterns Court arose on the site of a small farmhouse known as Whitefields or Posterns House just south of Wymbletons. General Charles 'Chinese' Gordon (of Khartoum) stayed there with his sister, Elizabeth Dunlop, and her husband, whilst home from the army on leave. (When later owned by Frederick S Philips it was renamed Sunnyside). And in the north Sir Joseph Boehm built himself an even more impressive mansion. Bentsbrook, situated a little to the south of the old pottery at North Holmwood, backed on to open farmland. It was, by the standards of the late nineteenth century, a splendid modern mansion, packed full of the latest designs in furniture and Arts and Crafts style interior decor.

Art and Inspiration in Holmwood – Sir Joseph Edgar Boehm, Christopher Whall and William Biscombe Gardener

Born in Vienna of a Hungarian family the sculptor Sir Joseph Boehm built a studio on Spook Hill, opposite his mansion, Bentsbrook (above). He was much commissioned by Queen Victoria for whom he modeled John Brown, (who called him Mr Bum), and the royal dogs. London is dotted with his work: Disraeli at Westminster Abbey, Darwin at the Natural History Museum, General Gordon at St Pauls, the Duke of Wellington at Hyde Park Corner. He invited Whistler to Holmwood, sending him a railway timetable, and was close to the Queen's artist daughter, Princess Louise, ending his life in scandalous circumstances, alone with her in his Kensington studio when he died of a heart attack in 1890. Boehm's mansion survived until 1936. Its 13 acres now form Bentsbrook Park. Built on the site of some ancient dwellings known as Little Egypt, the Studio still stands, with its great wall of windows. In 1955 a plaster cast of Boehm's right hand was found in the garden of next-door Royston (now Nutcracker) Cottage. *(Surrey Archaeological Society)*

Boehm was not the only artist working in Holmwood. In 1885 Christopher Whall, a designer of windows for James Powell and Sons, moved to Ada Cottage on the Blackbrook road. There he kept a smallholding with his portrait-painter wife, Florence. Wishing to master the art of glass making, he set up studio in one of the outbuildings and completed his first major commission there. Perhaps significantly, his sister-in-law, Alice Chaplin, was another sculptor of animals patronised by Queen Victoria. Though he left for Dorking in the 1890s and thence to London (where, with his originality and inspirational craftsmanship, he became prominent in the Arts and Crafts movement, writing what is regarded as the best manual ever written on the subject), it was in Holmwood that he learned his craft. Whall's daughter, Veronica, born in Holmwood, also became a notable stained glass artist.

Drawing on the Common was a popular pastime for visitors and numerous sketches of the church were left at the vicarage in commemoration of happy stays. The Wickham girls painted and the Ladies Legge had a studio at Holmwood Lodge. They took lessons from Edwin Douglas, one of whose sketches raised £40 towards the endowment of the church at North Holmwood. The engraver William Biscombe Gardner made a series of engravings of picturesque Holmwood, including the scene above of Redlands Farm, for the 'English Illustrated Magazine' in the 1890s *(Westcott Local History Group)*

With the possibility of daily commuting the area was open to professionals whose business was in London. More modest family houses or 'villas' began to be built within a horse-taxi ride of the station: Redlands Bank, the Oaks and the Elms, the Dutch House, Rosedene and numerous others along the undulating road. Many of the new households were headed by women for the Holmwood was popular as a retirement destination for lawyers, military men, colonial servants and members of the Indian Army, professionals who arrived with their, generally considerably younger, wives who were often left widows not many years later. Other ladies of private means removed themselves to the country on widowhood, often with complete households of servants. Ladies' maids, parlour maids, kitchen maids, cooks and housemaids, footmen, butlers and coachmen: by the 1880s many of the larger houses had a dozen servants living in, not counting the gardeners, bailiffs and labourers in tied cottages.

By 1869 South Holmwood's school rooms which had been built for eighty were accommodating a hundred and twenty. The Charity Commissioners insisted upon a certificated master before advancing grant monies for enlargement: a pension was therefore raised for Mr Dolman and Joseph Bixby was appointed headmaster. The children in Mr Bixby's charge were divided into five classes, learning scripture, reading, the Bible, needlework, arithmetic, religious knowledge and singing, (the latter taught by Reverend Wickham's daughter, Julia). Separate playgrounds were introduced for boys and girls and in 1872 an infant teacher was appointed, followed by an assistant master. Two years later Major Rohde Hawkins of the Education Department arranged for the school to become a Church of England National school.

The school was run by the parish and administered by the local worthies. Set at 3d a week, (as long as the children took their turn at cleaning), fees remained problematic, however, notwithstanding a legacy from Mrs Larpent in 1879 and the fact that Lady MacDonald of the Knoll and the Misses Chaldecott of Eutrie House, (daughters of the Dorking doctor), were paying for a number of individuals. In 1891 the managers accepted the 'fee grant' of the Elementary Education Act and opened the school free of charge. Many

Built for the London barrister, John Lance, on the site of a beer-shop, Brook Lodge was home to Lieutenant Colonel Louis de Cetto of the Royal Artillery. Well connected, (one of his godparents was the King of Bavaria), he was a trustee of the Hope estate, and in the 1880s took legal action against the Duke of Newcastle (under-Lyme) to stem the sale of family heirlooms. With 12 bedrooms, a billiard room, two carriage drives, 9 acres of ornamental grounds and a small farm at Brook Lodge, De Cetto also had the 50 acre Waterland tenanted. *(Dorking Museum)*

The farmhouse that stood on the site of Church Terrace. It was painted in 1872, shortly before the development of South Holmwood swept it away. *(Dorking Museum)*

parents, however, remained indifferent to their children's attendance. Often the reasons were economic: every year attendance was low around hay making in June, at harvest time, and in August for whortleberry picking, fern cutting and acorn gathering. The school had also to contend with difficulties of access when there was snow on the ground, and if conditions were very bad it would close.

Illness also disrupted education. Children endured prolonged absences for whooping cough, measles, mumps, scarlet fever, flu, diphtheria and scarletina, even those not affected in a family being prohibited from attending for fear of spreading such diseases. In the scarlet fever outbreak of 1891 some children returned to school after twenty weeks off, and if disease was epidemic the school would be closed for weeks at a time, as during the measles and whooping cough epidemic of June 1885, when, after weeks of low attendance, the school was closed for a six week period. Then there were days off for local custom: on 1st May each year the children took garlands and may poles round the village and in June they took a day off for the Foresters' anniversary celebrations with further days awarded for school treats at Anstie Grange or at Oakdale and for events of national significance when sports days would be held.

There had been a school, a church, a mill and a string of businesses along the roadside and at the Common's fringes in 'South Holmwood' for thirty years. By the 1870s a small terrace – Spring Cottages – had gone up opposite the school and the area around the turnpike gate and Grandon Lodge had grown populous. The paddocks and orchards of the cottages along the road around the old dissenting chapel and the Holly and Laurel, (as the Sawyers' was now known), had also been built upon. In 1873 came the heart of what

Part of Willow Green was known as Chapel Cottages before the establishment of the church at North Holmwood. The small cottage – long demolished - in the foreground was the chapel. *(Eileen Fox)*

48

is now the village as the small farm once know as Cowpers, (between the church and the inn), was developed by speculators. The hundred plots were advertised as *an opportunity... to small capitalists for the safe and profitable investment of funds, to the builder as sites on which to erect small genteel residences which would readily let, or to the small proprietor desirous of building a residence for his own occupation, surrounded by the open expense of common with its magnificent views and bracing air, affording all the pleasure without the expense of maintenance attached to private pleasure grounds'* The plots became Church Terrace, Warwick, Norfolk and Buckingham Roads. The two and three bed-roomed houses built there were within walking distance of church and school, suitable for artisans and tradesmen who were not accommodated by the farms or estates. Some remained unbuilt, however, into the 1890s after the developer WJ Shearburn went bankrupt. In the meantime businesses established themselves in and around the new hub, amongst them Crofts', the fancy bread and biscuit makers, whose premises were next door to Steyning Cottage, and the rival baker and confectioner, Bates'.

On the northern fringes of the Common another community was developing. In 1871 the long defunct pottery, (together with the lowly cottages that stood upon it), was sold in lots. A row of small, workmanlike dwellings went up in its place. The ribbon of development along the roadside between the brow of Spook Hill and the Norfolk Arms was now much extended and the area so populous that in 1874 the parochial district of North Holmwood district was created. (It became a full parish - as South Holmwood - in 1878.) Everything north of Redlands Lane and Mid Holmwood Lane, (more or less the land that had been transferred into Holmwood with the formation of Coldharbour twenty years earlier), was transferred into the new district.

The church of St John the Divine was designed by Mr Hawkins and situated on land once again donated by the Duke. Its principal benefactors were the elderly Ladies Anne and Mary Legge, daughters of the 3rd Earl of Dartmouth, who lived at Holmwood Lodge where they held fundraising bazaars and sales of work. It was consecrated on Easter Day 1875 and a year later the Legges, the architect and the Rev Thomas Henry Waters, (whose ministry is commemorated in a window of 1892 by Charles Eamer Kempe), planted trees around the churchyard.

Designed by Major Rohde Hawkins of Redlands, the church of St John the Evangelist is built of flint in a style derivative of Early English, its tower topped by a spire.
The glass panels in the east window are by James Powell and Sons of London.

The parish's second vicar, the Reverend Somerset Lowry, who served from 1891 to 1900, wrote several well-known hymns including *'A man there lived in Galilee'.*

North Holmwood School

North Holmwood School. *(Dorking Museum/Des Scutt)*

In the 1880s and 90s further development, particularly around the Norfolk area seemed likely as a second railway line through Holmwood was repeatedly in prospect which might have brought a station to Mid Holmwood. After years of prevarication the LBSCR drew up plans to extend a line south from Box Hill in 1897 to run west of Dorking and Holmwood Common, passing behind the Norfolk and St Mary Magdalene then down to Cranleigh and Midhurst. This proposal met with opposition, however, from the people of Dorking who wanted a competing line operated by the rival LSWR. Concerns were also expressed that the new line would bring day trippers *'with broken bottles, meat tins and sandwich papers after their manner,'* to the Common, which together with Redlands Wood, would become *'more like Ashtead Common'*. Nothing came, either, of the Holmwood, Cranleigh, Midhurst and Havant Railway Company's proposal to link Holmwood into a direct line from London to Portsmouth[18].

With the split in the parochial districts South Holmwood's infant outpost became the new district's school. In 1874 there were 116 on the roll. Soon it was over a hundred, and by 1889 the number had grown to 225. Attendance, however, was still erratic, as the headmaster noted: *' Many are away in consequence of work and other valid excuses but the apathy of parents allows a great deal of irregularity and makes the teachers long for more stringent acts of compulsion.'* At North Holmwood children were absent for perhaps an even greater range of reasons than their cohort in the south: mothers needing help with lodgers during the summer season, cherry watching, bracken cutting, hop picking and cover beating, not to mention the pantomime, the circus and the Band of Hope outing. The Rev Wickham called on parents, offering rewards for regular attendance, and when attendance became compulsory he reported to the attendance officer weekly, not necessarily with great success: in February 1896 the parents of Elizabeth and John Upward were fined for their children having attended on thirteen of a possible 146 occasions!

Not that the headmasters always welcomed compulsory attendance: in 1878 South Holmwood's head was complaining about the re-admittance of a 'totally ignorant' child under pressure from the attendance committee since he *'must remain a drag on school work.'* Similarly with Frederick Booker who was readmitted in 1879 under a magistrate's order: *'an ignorant lad, of very unruly habits... it will be well for the rest of the children*

---

[18] Tantalisingly, Alan Jackson suggests that the route would have offered an alternative to the Dorking road bypass which desecrated The Deepdene in 1931, an event which in its turn led to the A24's destruction of the Holmwood villages several decades later; Jackson, Alan A.: *Dorking's Railways*, Dorking, 1988 p47

when he becomes of legal age to leave'. Full attendance also gave rise to accommodation problems: the school was enlarged in 1883 but soon afterwards the infants, of whom there were now 90, were being housed in two galleries.

Instruction, particularly for the girls, was basic and utilitarian: the inspectors complained in 1874 that there were no specimens in darning and patching and no instruction was being given in knitting. The new Education Code curriculum of the 1890s only marginally improved the range of studies, it mainly consisting of reading, writing and religion, with history being reserved for the boys. The school's marching, however, was 'tolerably fair', noted the inspectors in 1892.

The children got up to the usual mischief: one truant of the 1870s, Sidney Knight, was described by the headmaster as: *'a very bad boy indeed... Perhaps fortunately he is about the most irregular in the school otherwise his evil influence would be more appreciable.'* One less than sharp lad, Stephen Davey, was caught out having faked a note asking to be allowed to leave at three on being caught outside birds-nesting at 3.35! Punishment was physical and not always without parental objection: in 1879 the parents of one boy threatened Mr Bixby with a summons for assault after he punished their son. Cruelty to bats, pushing one another into ponds or ditches, throwing stones at ducks, throwing mud, lighting fires on the Common, as well as the usual misdemeanours of smoking, whistling and rudeness, all met with the headmasters' attention.

The antiquarian John Gough Nichols bought Holmwood House in 1866 and renamed it Holmwood Park. Scholar, writer, editor and publisher of the influential 'Gentleman's Magazine', he was a member of an illustrious publishing family and moved in the same cultured and intellectual circles as the Larpents and the Heaths, indeed his grandfather John Nichols had had his portrait engraved by Charles Heath, half-brother of George Heath of Kitlands. A founder member of a number of learned societies and prolific historical writer, when John Gough Nichols died in 1873 Holmwood Park was home to one of the greatest collections of historical and topographical books of its time most of which is now held by Leicester University. *(Photograph Centre for English Local History Studies, University of Leicester)*

Imports of foreign foodstuffs may have been affecting farm prices by the end of the century, putting many small farms out of business, but in Holmwood the effects were mitigated by the number of farms that had been subsumed into the great estates and by increased employment opportunities off the land. The management of the Common, however, proceeded much as it had in medieval times. Cows and horses still roamed, keeping vegetation cover low, and most houses kept a few animals. Goats remained prohibited. Nonetheless some still sought to run them: in 1883 notice was given to a number of commoners that their goats must be removed. Charles Smith's two goats and three kids were impounded in May of the following year. When not redeemed they were sold but the balance raised after the auctioneer's costs came to less than the costs of impounding them. Enforcement action was not always economically viable.

Though the Common continued to be a valuable resource, it was surrounded by a massively increased population, many of whom treated it as a garden centre. Hollies were frequently taken and in the 1880s, after it was alleged that a Mr Butcher had dug up thirty-five bushes, a charge was instituted of 3d per bush should hollies be replanted on the Common or a shilling should they be planted on private land. The levy did not stop the thefts, however.

Holly was not the only thing being plundered: in 1884 the brick maker James Edwards was pursued for cutting oaks and in 1886 Mr Rapley, the surveyor for the Highway Board, was accused of taking turf from the roadside at Blackbrook. Others dug sawpits in it and drainage ditches over it, stored building materials on it and hung out clothes to dry there. They stockpiled manure, put their fence supports, pig styes, sheds and outhouses on it. The Batchelors of the Pig and String ale-house, (later known as the Volunteer, just north of the Royal Oak at Stonebridge), even created an unauthorised pond on it in 1885. They were also adept at exploiting common law: when challenged about an unauthorised shed the builder and landlord of the Norfolk, Charles Pierce, claimed a long established right. The Duchy had, therefore, to be vigilant even in minor matters, requiring written acknowledgements even in respect of temporary incursions to prevent the surreptitious assumption of rights.

With such numerous assaults the medieval system of regulation was, by the late nineteenth century, proving unsatisfactory. There were tensions, not just between the Duchy and those exploiting the Common, but between the Duchy and the wealthier of those living in and about it. The Duke's priority was to rein in expenditure on land that now brought in little income whilst many living nearby wanted to see increased expenditure on the maintenance of paths and ponds, often for purely aesthetic reasons. Therefore the Holmwood Common General Committee, a volunteer body funded by local subscription and made up of the usual grandees who reported to and took their instructions from the Duke, was set up in 1883. One of its first acts was to recruit a common keeper, Sergeant Atkins, who was delegated to cut the hollies required by the churches or the furzes allowed to local bonfire committees.

The work of the Committee and of the Duke's steward was time consuming. Miscreants required warnings and threats and though the Committee relieved the Duke of the day to day management of the Common he did not fund it. This made enforcement action virtually impossible. Nor did he devolve much in the way of power: anything of a serious nature, or which might give rise to a precedent or establish a right, had to be referred back to his agent. The unprecedented pressures which the Common now faced, at a time when funds coming in were low, lead to conflict. After a dispute in 1888, however, the Duke agreed to subscribe to the Committee's costs at a percentage of total subscriptions.

Since its establishment the church, and the Duke, had run the Holmwood but with the growth of local democracy the power of the parish, like that of the Lord, was waning. Neither parish nor local worthy was any longer responsible for the roads. In 1880 the turnpike was wound up, its final term expired. Holmwood's gates, posts, ironwork and lanterns were sold at auction. Responsibility for the roads now fell to the district council's highway board. In taking over the parish rates, (which had replaced the obligation on parishioners to labour on the road), integration and cooperation was possible over a wider area than when each road was owned and maintained by small independent parishes. Full-time engineers and road builders could be employed, who were able to use new techniques, rather than piecemeal tenders and contracts. Mr Alloway, the rate collector for the Highway District of Dorking, worked on commission. Mr Rapley, the highways' surveyor, lived at Mid Holmwood and kept the Board's steam roller.

The new District Council also intervened in landowners' affairs in a way that the parish never had: in the 1890s it required that Hallswell Spring at North Holmwood be cleared and fenced, that an impassable footpath at the rear of the Norfolk Arms be cleared, that a stile be repaired between Folly Farm and Betchets Green, and that a nailed-up gate be opened between Holmwood Cottage and Holmwood Park. Wrangling with the Duke's agent about costs inevitably followed. Wrangling also took place when the town authorities sought to impose more lavish plans upon the Common for the worthies of Dorking regarded the

The Plough at Blackbrook began life as a cottage. With a wheelwright's then a smithy on site, the inn and its brew house were run from the 1850s by the Elphick family who continued to run it into the 20th century. Like the Norfolk, its clientele in the late 19th century was 'a low class of person'.

Holmwood as something of a wasteland, ideal for the siting of such facilities as were not suitable for the town. In 1878 it was proposed that an isolation hospital be sited on the Common where patients with contagious diseases – in particular smallpox - might be contained away from the rest of the community. Opposition was so great, however, that the proposal was shelved. Similarly an 'inebriate reformatory' was proposed for the Holmwood in the 1890s.

In 1890 a mission room was established at South Holmwood with money left by Lady MacDonald, (supplemented by the Reverend Wickham). This played the role of a village hall and by the end of the century the parish was running a Mothers' Union, the Band of Hope, coal and clothing clubs, a library and temperance society. Alternative social and welfare providers were appearing on the scene, however.

From 1866 there had been a village hospital in Capel to which contributions were made from church collections and the vicar's wife sat on the committee of the Bertha Broadwood Nursing Association to which a number of Holmwood households subscribed. The Oddfellows, (who had established themselves in Dorking in 1844), set up a Holmwood lodge at the Holly and Laurel in 1855. The rival Ancient Order of Foresters established the Robin Hood 'court' in 1869, meeting in an upstairs room at the Norfolk Arms until Charles Taylor, (who took over as landlord from his father-in-law, Charles Pierce, in 1882), re-erected a temporary church building from Mickleham at the back of the inn in 1898. These societies, which raised funds through subscription to be used by members in time of need, marked a move towards self reliance by the vulnerable. They also provided companionship to the many who were new to the Holmwood, for, although their purpose was

The Foresters on parade with drums and banners outside the late Georgian/early Victorian Norfolk Arms before its extension and remodelling at the beginning of the 20th century gave it another wing, a pitched roof and bay windows. *(Eileen Fox)*

53

insurance against misfortune at a time when there was no health service, no old age pension and no sick pay, they were renowned for their social events. Every year on the first Sunday in September the Foresters held a church parade which was attended by courts from miles around. Members marched with banners and in full regalia from the Norfolk to St Mary Magdalene then returned for tea in the 'big-room'.

The inns were part meeting house, association headquarters, social gathering place and, in the case of the Holly and Laurel, sports pavilion. With their patches of common before them where meetings could be held and processions gathered, they were at the heart of vibrant communities. In July the Holly and Laurel hosted Pledge's Fair with coconut shies, a circus tent, boxing and freak shows whilst Taylor's Fair was held at the Norfolk. The inns also played host on occasions of national celebration: the Holly and Laurel was the focus of celebrations for Queen Victoria's Golden Jubilee in 1887 when a bonfire and fireworks were held on the Common opposite. Ten years later the Diamond Jubilee was celebrated there with sports and tea for three hundred children.

It was at the station, however, that the people of Holmwood paid their last respects to their Queen, standing bare-headed beside the line as her funeral train passed on its way from the Isle of Wight to London in the second year of the new century.

The end of Holmwood mill

The mill remained in Edward Swan's family from 1775 until 1867 when John Bishop, descendent of his daughter, Lucy, emigrated to America, sending back instructions for its sale in the early 1870s. The reliability of watermills - several of which had become accessible to local people with improvements in the roads - put windmills at a disadvantage and when it fell into disrepair the cost of maintenance proved uneconomic. In 1873 the mill was purchased by Thomas Henry Rumbold, a London barrister, and replaced with a grand residence. *(Dorking Museum)*

Oakdene, Four Wents and the Duke of Cambridge's Review

In 1876 the Duke of Cambridge, uncle of Queen Victoria and Commander-in-Chief of the British Army, reviewed over three thousand militiamen in the grounds of Oakdene. Six hundred members of the Perthshire Regiment under the command of Lord Stormont, 750 of the Renfrewshire Regiment under the command of Sir Robert Napier and a thousand of the Wigton Regiment under the command of Lord Galloway arrived by train that July, some of them miners who had been encouraged to join the militia to obtain sunlight for a couple of months in the summer. For twelve days they trained and camped high on the Common to the east of the road and to the south of North Holmwood church. Eight hundred members of the Armagh (Irish) militia under Lord Lurgan camped further south, on the hill between the Black Brook and the Holly and Laurel.

Canteens were set up to supply beer, with eighteen hundred loaves being delivered each day and seven beasts slaughtered daily. Four Wents, previously a small pond, was enlarged to water the horses. A tented reading room was also provided and many of the men attended services at Holmwood church. One of them, an elderly Army Service Corps follower, was buried there. On the day of the inspection the troops were marched west to Oakdene, each regiment accompanied by a water cart as men were passing out in the heat. The following day camp was struck and the troops went off by train to Guildford and thence to Aldershot. *(Photographs by permission of Surrey History Centre)*

Cricket, fairs and church parades

Holmwood and the Boer War

Three of Sir Leopold's five sons made careers in the services. Admiral Sir Herbert (right) became Second Sea Lord. General Sir Gerard Moore Heath (left) won the DSO during the Boer War following the siege of Ladysmith. Frederick Crofton Heath, then a lieutenant, was also mentioned in dispatches.

In 1903 Captain Manning, son of Holmwood's police sergeant, was met at Holmwood Station on his return from the war by Sir Leopold, the headmaster and a flag-waving crowd in celebration of his DSO. Other Holmwood boys fared less well: Charles Austin died at Colenso where Alf Worsfold and F. Sayers were wounded. Acting-Corporal S Higgins was killed at Pieters Hill. *(JJ Heath Caldwell)*

The new cottage next to the Old Nag's was named Mafeking (Redcott) on the relief of the siege there.

By the turn of the twentieth century the building of mansions had largely come to an end. Villas were still being built, however, and cottages upgraded, particularly where the Common bounded Inholms. There smallholdings remained with the potential for gardens of several acres. At Brookmeadow the cottage in the orchard was given a tile-hung façade and a new wing in the 1890s by Mr Ball, a London accountant. Littlebrook Farm made way for a house with a sweeping new access.

Nearby Bellevue and Laurel Cottage were incorporated into Holmwood House and Daisy Cottage was

NORTH HOLMWOOD COMMON

At North Holmwood the grass was close cropped and at the pond there were no willows, rushes or reeds but it was a bleak pool, scuffed at the edges and devoid of vegetation, the result of constant pressure from the feet of drinking animals. A row of willows, (some of which remain), lead up to Holmwood Lodge with a spur off to the row of cottages then known as Holmesdale Terrace. *(Mary Day)*

Mary Ann Peters established a grocery at Mid Holmwood in the 1850s. From the 1880s Edward and Emma Bond and various of their ten children ran the bakery and general store there.

transformed by the wool-broker, Angelus Beyfus into Daisy Lodge.

Up at the roadside development was less grand. Terraces and villas went up around the Norfolk and behind Holmesdale House whilst, on the other side of the road, Brook Valley replaced the cottage gardens behind the Old Nag's and brick villas went up at the roadside. The inn was now surrounded by businesses – several shops, the landlord's carrying and vehicle hire, the Pierces' building and undertaking trade, Mr Batchelor's wheelright's premises and Isemonger's walking stick and umbrella handle factory. Isemonger's was a sizable operation employing a number of men. Obtaining wood from the Barclays' plantations, Isemonger disposed of his shavings into the Norfolk pond. Wood dealing also provided Samson Davey and his family of nearby Redlands Cottages with a living. Smallholdings remained, however, even in this industrious area: Ernest Bond, (whose parents ran the store), rented the farmyard at Holmesdale House and turned out nine or ten cows onto the Common. There they mingled with Mr Arthur's geese from Mafeking, with Mr Robertson's cattle and sheep from Littlebrook and with Mr Kelsey's pigs from the Nag's.

The inn had a somewhat rough clientele, despite the parish of St Mary Magdalene having established a mission room staffed by Church Army ministers at Brook Valley. In an attempt to persuade parishioners away from the inn the mission room, which hosted clubs, social events and 'coffee suppers', moved in 1909 into a hut next to Priory Cottage and began to open in the evenings as a men's reading room. The Norfolk, however, remained home to the Foresters and host to meetings of local and national import.

Harry Isemonger's factory. A lay preacher whose family had been in the area since the 17th century, Isemonger lived nearby at the Promised Land (Solway House) where he held prayer meetings at the chapel in his garden. On the same site 'Blondin' Batchelor (whose sign is to the left) operated as a wheelwright and carpenter. The Norfolk Garage now stands on the site. (Eileen Fox)

The Norfolk Arms – Pierce, Taylor and Worrow

In the 1870s the Norfolk's landlord was Charles Field Pierce whose family building business, run from the inn, was responsible for developing much of Mid Holmwood. He was followed in the 1880s by his son-in-law, Charles Taylor, who had married his daughter, Minnie. When Taylor died in 1908 the tenancy went to a relative who had often holidayed in Holmwood, Issac 'Jack' Worrow from London. Taylor's fly, horse-taxi and stabling business went to Minnie's brother, Frank Pierce, the building and undertaking business to another brother, Walter Pierce. Under the Worrows the inn was renovated, its Georgian exterior 'Victorianised', with a new porch and a bayed extension, its roof given a steeper pitch. The Worrows lived across the road at Redcott. In the above photograph Jack Worrow is shown as a child with his sisters outside the Norfolk holding the donkey. The lady beside him is probably Minnie Taylor, daughter of Charles and Susannah Field Pierce. *(Eileen Fox)*

The last of the great houses – Minnickfold and Rough Rew

Minnickfold (left) - a mock-Tudor confection constructed in 1898 on eighteen acres purchased from the Moorhurst estate – was one of the last of Holmwood's grand houses to be constructed. *(Dorking Museum)*

Between North Holmwood and Dorking and bordering Holmwood Farm, Rough Rew (right) was built in 1913 by Robert Memphis Aitken and stood in forty-two acres. In 1948 it became the regional headquarters of the South Eastern Electricity Board. *Painting by Agnes Ruff. (Dorking Museum)*

With the upgrading of smallholdings fewer households made agricultural demands on the Common. It now faced different threats, however. Many of the mansions had lowly origins within the Common and insufficient land for lawns, tennis courts and lodges. The only way that they could be expanded was by the acquisition of adjacent common land but as commoners had rights the Duke of Norfolk could not simply sell. Instead wealthy owners would buy land adjoining the Common elsewhere, throw it out 'unto common', (so making it available for use), being permitted in return to enclose an equivalent area adjacent to their gardens. The process began in the 1880s when John Vivian Hampton and his wife, Lady

Laura, enlarged Oakdale, (throwing open an old enclosure near Four Wents and another near Mill Bottom). Bellevue, the Elms and Furzelea (Moorfield) were all thus enlarged and the process continued into the new century at Mill House, the Old Croft, Ferndale Cottage, Holmwood Lodge, Rosedene and Woodlands Park. The favoured area for acquisition was at Inholms adjoining Brookmeadow where half a dozen strips that had been farmland for hundreds of years were opened to common.

The Holly and Laurel with charabancs. *(Des Scutt)*

The depletion of such commons as Holmwood, however, was becoming a matter of wider than local concern: in 1911 the Commons and Footpaths Preservation Society opposed proposals for further enclosures. Local interests now vied with those of outsiders as guidebooks extolled the virtues of the Surrey Hills, in particular the walk from the station up Leith Hill, described as *'one of the most romantic hillsides in England'* by one writer. Cyclists and motorbus parties now joined those arriving by rail and local inns were recommended as refreshment stops. The White Hart, the Holly and Laurel and the Norfolk all offered tea gardens and accommodation whilst many householders let rooms. In 1906 even the great vicarage was let for the summer with the vicar moving into the Elms opposite the Norfolk. Thereafter it was regularly let.

The Holmwoods were thriving. Farms employed scores as did local businesses which supplied groceries to the mansions, serviced their vehicles and shod their horses. Residences like Oakdene, Holmwood Park, Anstie Grange and Kitlands had attic rooms for a dozen live-in staff, plus gardeners' cottages and accommodation for coachmen and drivers over garages and stables, but they also employed vast numbers on a daily basis and many cottagers took in laundry or undertook dressmaking. So in awe were local people of such as the Heaths, though, that they curtseyed and touched their caps when they met.

Some of the grand houses, however, were beginning to be adversely affected by developments. Bentsbrook, (as North Holmwood now tended to be known), in particular, was no longer a quiet backwater. The brickyard which had begun at Stubs Farm in the 1880s was now in the hands of the Dorking Brick Company which had worked from Rushets to the east of the Newdigate road until 1901. With demand high the brickworks expanded. Spawning a terraced estate on its approach behind Willow Green, its workings were creeping up on retired Lieutenant Colonel Edward Legge, (nephew of Ladies Anne and Mary), his wife Cordelia, and their family of siblings, step-siblings, governesses and servants at Holmwood Lodge. Increased traffic brought business opportunities, however, to roadside properties. One of the pot-kiln cottages had sold produce via a makeshift shop to passers-by since the 1890s whilst the occupants of another traded vegetables from a rack. Now the rack was superseded by a covered stall and the North Holmwood Cabin was in business. It later added a tea garden whilst next door Frost's took to the sale of tea, flour and groceries, the village post office relocating there from its home across the green.

The main road was surfaced now with chalk and flint and flattened by steam roller. The council also took responsibility for key routes like Warwick and Buckingham roads, the frontagers contributing towards the cost of bringing them up to local authority standards. Most of Holmwood's tracks remained the responsibility of owners and occupiers, however, and with increased usage some were in deplorable condition: in 1909 tenants from Redlands Cottages had to wade ankle deep in mud to the main road. With the cost of repairs beyond their means the situation was only rectified when the Surveyor of Highways, Mr Rapley, offered his services with the roller and Mrs Secretan raised the funds for materials to enable cottagers to undertake repairs.

Though the Nichols of Holmwood Park kept seven horses until the start of the First World War, many of Holmwood's wealthy were making the change from horse to motor power: by 1914 the Pethick Lawrences kept three cars at the Mascot, several other households had a couple and a score at least one. Most, however, were not so blessed: South Holmwood cricket team borrowed wagons from Mr Hoad or from Frank Pierce for away games whilst the fire brigade relied upon the Hoads' horses. Horse buses, operating from the Windmill Inn on Flint Hill, took villagers into Dorking. Attempts to replace these in 1903 with Heasman's motor bus (which ran from the Holly and Laurel through Dorking to the station) met with limited success: so taxing was the gradient that passengers often had to get off and push. A rival service run by Mr Swift of the Three Tuns in Dorking lasted but a year; another in 1909 survived only months. By 1913, however, there was a motorised service three times daily from Dorking station and in 1914 a route was introduced by East Surrey Traction Company from Brockham Green and the Holly and Laurel via Dorking station using a double-decker Daimler.

But if the bus fare into Dorking was too expensive practically everything a family might need could be obtained in Holmwood itself. To the north of Steyning Cottage Cyprus Villa housed a shop; next to the Holly and Laurel was Barker the butcher, and at the station West's, the tea merchant and general supplier, with another bread and biscuit baker, Bates', nearby. Further north John Jenkins kept a general store near the Norfolk and Henry Davey another in addition to Bonds'. A few hundred yards further north was Frank Butcher's bakery at Rosewood Cottage. Milk from local farms, coal from the station, bread from Crofts', feed from Attlee's in Dorking and groceries from Kingham's – all were delivered.

Holiday charabancs, buses, delivery vehicles: there was traffic in the Holmwoods. As early as 1906 children at North Holmwood were warned of the dangers of playing in the road and on 29th September 1913 the villages suffered their first motorized vehicle fatality when Lily Tobitt, aged 13, was run over and killed outside South Holmwood School.

Barker's delivery bike. In the early years of the 20th century Walter Barker was Holmwood's butcher, employing a large staff at his premises next to the Holly and Laurel. He was also the tenant of Folly Farm, where other family members were employed. The shop survived until 2006. *(Dorking Museum)*

Save for the dangers the increase in road traffic had little effect on the lives of many Holmwood villagers. Leisure time continued to be spent on the Common and in the villages. Partly in consequence of prevailing negative attitudes towards alcohol it was decided to establish a club in South Holmwood in commemoration of the coronation of Edward VII. The site selected was that of the Warwick

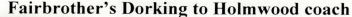

Fairbrother's Dorking to Holmwood coach

D. Fairbrother & Sons, The Windmill, Flint Hill, Dorking.

Daniel Fairbrother's Dorking to Holmwood double-decker horse-bus operated from the Windmill on Flint Hill. Landlord of the inn, Fairbrother also farmed Goodwyns. His bus met with an accident on a Saturday morning in 1903 when nearly all the passengers – 'bean feasters' visiting Holmwood – refused to come down from the upper deck, despite its being top heavy, causing the bus to sway and swerve until the load became too much for the horses. The driver jumped from his box, the bus ran up a bank and overturned. Two people were taken to Capel cottage hospital with serious injuries. In the 1970s the carcass of the bus was found in a field being lived in by a tramp. After restoration it took a trip through Dorking in 1985. *(Des Scutt)*

Road mission room. Plans went ahead despite the objections of the cricketer and developer, Wildman Cattley who had built a number of substantial houses on the roadside nearby which he felt would be detrimentally affected. Mr Pethick Lawrence donated a billiard table and in 1904 a bottle containing a newspaper and coins was placed under the dedication stone when Mrs Bosworth Smith, daughter of the late Rev Wickham, laid the first stone. With its coffee bar serving teas to hikers – no alcohol was to be served – the club proved so popular that membership had to be regulated, it being impossible to accommodate everyone.

On the Common cricket had been long established and in 1909 South Holmwood was a founder members of the Dorking and District Football League. Nor did the Holmwood lack for less gentle sport: the Warnham stag hounds turned out at Inholms or at Holmwood Lodge with Mr Hack entertaining at the Knoll beforehand whilst the local gentry hunted with the Surrey Union hounds and the Duke let shooting rights on Redlands woods.

The educational ways of the twentieth century were brought to South Holmwood with the sudden death of Mr Bixby in 1906. On her retirement the following year Mrs Bixby received thirty-seven sovereigns, one for each year of her service. The new headmaster, Mr Fayers, transformed the school into a modern establishment. Adopting the motto, *'Have no slackness'*, he put in a drill ground and vegetable gardens, instituted prizes, and formed a cricket club. Numbers were falling, however, with only 170 on the books and fewer in attendance. Built when fewer were attending and with limited ambition, the Holmwood schools struggled to comply with government demands for more teachers, for physical exercise, for the division of classrooms or for more of them. After six years Mr Fayers resigned. His replacement was Arthur Lay.

Cricket on the Common

The Duke of Norfolk allowed temporary enclosure of the Common for cricket in 1864 and when headmaster Bixby died in 1906 he had been secretary of the village cricket club in South Holmwood for thirty-two years. The playing area was enclosed with a post and chain fence, the pavilion was a tent, few players could afford whites and matches could only be played on bank holidays or Saturday afternoons. With teas served at the Holly and Laurel, however, a trip to Holmwood was a day out for opposing teams At North Holmwood a sports club was established in 1908 and in 1909 workmen from Anstie Grange who were lodging in South Holmwood also had a team.
William, the son of the Rev Inge, played cricket for Oxford University, as had the sons of Rev Wickham before him. Stephen Wildman Cattley, the hop dealer who briefly owned Oakdene in the 1880s and who developed a number of properties at the roadside in South Holmwood (including the Dutch House), played for Surrey in the 1880s and was an early treasurer of Surrey County Cricket Club. A later treasurer there was George Henry Longman (of the publishing firm) who lived at Holmwood Cottage and who was master of the Surrey Union Hunt in the early years of the century, then chairman of Holmwood's defence committee during the First World War. *(Dorking Museum)*

Despite the growing infrastructure many families were still but a few steps from poverty: during the miners' strike of 1912 the Duke of Norfolk allowed wood to be cut on the Common when coal prices grew prohibitive and the vicarage ran coal and clothing clubs. The Foresters grew both more popular and more sophisticated: labourers and artisans, gardeners, grooms, footmen and grocers almost universally joined as soon as they turned sixteen, many having been juvenile members, and in 1912 a women's section was proposed. Based at the Norfolk and run by Jack Worrow with the Pierces next door the Society now also advanced money on the security of mortgages in addition to the usual mutual insurance services, providing a community banking service. The mutual benefit ethos also extended into other areas enabling many to club together to provide services that none could afford alone: in 1900 South Holmwood began to employ a district nurse whose wages were raised by subscription. So successful was the scheme that a second nurse was engaged to cover North Holmwood and Blackbrook. Soon Holmwood was also subscribing towards a fire brigade.

The Common had long been subject to conflagration in the summer. North Holmwood boys were often reprimanded for lighting fires and the Beare Green Prosecuting

Sir Leopold and Cuthbert Heath at Anstie Grange

The close relationship between the Heaths and the parish of South Holmwood came to an end when, a few years before his death in 1907, Admiral Sir Leopold clashed with the Reverend Gill over some candles donated to St Mary Magdalene by Lady Laura Hampton of Oakdale. When the vicar refused to remove the 'ritualistic ornaments' from the altar Sir Leopold pointed out that he was the patriarch of the church, his father having been a major subscriber, and his brother-in-law having paid for the north aisle. To no avail. The dispute grew bitter with accusations flying in the local paper and provocative sermons.

Sir Leopold instituted a house-to-house canvass for signatures to petition the Ecclesiastical Commissioners and though he won his case relations between the two men were irreparably damaged. Thereafter the Heath family worshipped at Coldharbour.

On his brother Douglas Denon's death in 1897 Sir Leopold had leased Kitlands to his son Cuthbert. Prevented by deafness from following his brothers into the forces, Cuthbert had been set up with an insurance syndicate at Lloyds where he made a huge fortune. In the course of his career he transformed not just Lloyds but the whole insurance business. Pioneering non-marine markets, he was the first to offer insurance against burglary and issued the first American motor insurance policy. Wealthy enough to buy Anstie, his later acquisitions of the Duke's Warren on Leith Hill and of Redlands Wood brought the Heath estates to well over a thousand acres.

At Anstie Cuthbert hunted with the Surrey Union and held shooting parties whilst his wife, Caroline, presided over dances with formal processions into white tie dinners. At its most brilliant the house was like a small village with gardeners, stablemen, chauffeurs and a score of servants in the house itself. But whereas Douglas Denon had walked every day over to Anstie, the houses under Cuthbert and his brother Arthur Raymond, who came to Kitlands from Ewhurst in 1915, were never so close. *(Dorking Museum)*

Society paid its last reward in 1912 for information leading to a conviction for setting fire to the Common. In such events word was sent to the Dorking brigade by bicycle but after two serious fires in the spring of 1909 during the course of which a barn and stack at Breakspeares and many acres of common burned, the Holmwood brigade was formed. A public meeting brought forth volunteers, with the usual grandees – Mr Aguet of Mill House, Mr Hack of the Knoll Mrs Helsham Jones and Mr Pethick Lawrence - supplying most of the funds. With a fire engine drawn by horses from Mr Hoad's stables Chief Fire Officer Spencer Secretan, (a Lloyds underwriter of Langholm Cottage), drilled his volunteers every Tuesday night. Emergency calls came in to the post office and volunteers were called by means of a wind-up siren, boys fetching those who lived or worked too far away to hear it. Expenses were recovered from the owners of properties attended - 1s 6d an hour per fireman and 9d for succeeding hours. The brigade's annual fund-raising sports day with hose target competition on the cricket green was a highlight of the village calendar.

Save for the Foresters, which was run by small businessmen, local committees - for the village club, sports club, brigade or one-off celebration - were dominated by the denizens of the grand houses: the Secretans, the Heaths, the

Holmwood's fire brigade outside Mr Pierce's premises next to the Norfolk. The fire engine was kept in a shed next to the Crofts' post office rented from Hannah Pledge of the Holly and Laurel. *(Dorking Museum)*

Hacks, Habershons and Helsham Joneses. But it was no longer wealthy incomers handing down charity to impoverished indigents: with the establishment of clubs, benevolent institutions and subscription services the scattered cottages, artisans' terraces and grand mansions of the Holmwoods had become communities.

These years were the heyday of village life. In 1902 a dinner for the elderly and widowed was held to celebrate the coronation of Edward VII, followed by sports, dancing, and a bonfire. The celebration held in June 1911 for the coronation of his son, George V, was probably Holmwood's biggest ever. Frank Pierce's horses took the North Camberwell Military Band from the station to the Norfolk from whence it marched with the Oddfellows, Foresters, boy scouts and fire brigades to St Mary Magdalene. After dining at the Norfolk the band played for the pensioners' and widows' dinner at the Holly and Laurel, and at the childrens' tea when bread and butter, buns and cake were served to 200. Races were run all afternoon, then the band played, Mrs Habershon gave out the prizes and the bonfire was lit on this last great celebration before the war to end all wars.

A plane down in Holmwood

On July 3rd 1911 an aeroplane came down at Holmwood Farm, behind North Holmwood School. Its French pilot, Monsieur Gilbert, was taking part in the Circuit of Europe air race and had set off from Shoreham bound for Hendon. A chef was brought from the Falkland Arms to translate for him, boys absented themselves from school and crowds turned out to watch repairs carried out. The plane was then pulled from behind the school up the hill past the church to the cricket field in order to take off, its wings having to be removed in order to manoeuvre it up the bends and gradients of the lane to Inholms. *(Dorking Museum)*

Literary Holmwood –
Wilson Carlisle, E. Arnot Robertson
and 'the Balliol Bugger'

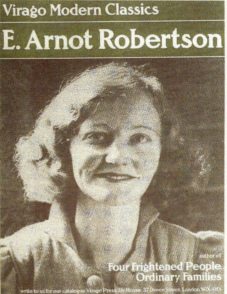

Wilson Carlisle, (left), founder of the Church Army, lived for many years off Chart Lane. While his house was being built, however, he stayed at North Holmwood's vicarage in Inholms Lane, during which time he often preached at St John's. *(Dorking Advertiser)*

The novelist, critic and broadcaster E. Arnot Robertson, (right), who spent her childhood at Templeton off Mill Road, was the daughter of Holmwood's first doctor. In the 1930s she became a literary sensation with her best-selling novels. (In the introduction to one she recalled her idyllic Holmwood childhood.) Her works were amongst the earliest to deal with sexual issues from a woman's perspective and caused some debate in literary circles. Her criticism was stringent: so detrimental did MGM consider her film reviews that the company tried to bar her from screenings of its films, an action which lead to protracted action in the courts. In the 1950s and 60s she was known for her radio appearances on 'Oh My Word!' with Dennis Norden and Frank Muir. *(Poster courtesy of Virago Press)*

One of St Mary Magdalene's most striking memorial windows is to the poet and novelist William Money Hardinge whose involvement with Walter Pater whilst an undergraduate at Balliol College in 1874 lead to the poet being denied a proctorship in an episode that for many years mystified scholars. Hardinge was accused by Benjamin Jowett, the Master of Balliol, of having written and disseminated immoral sonnets celebrating homosexual love. Investigation lead to the discovery of compromising letters from Pater to Hardinge who became known as the 'Balliol Bugger'. His predicament in late Victorian Oxford has inspired more than one literary representation, most notably the unnamed 'Balliol Student' in Tom Stoppard's 'The Invention of Love.'

'Votes for Women' and the 'Holmwood Campaign'

From 1901 to 1920 the Dutch House opposite Mill Road in South Holmwood played host to illustrious visitors: Olive Schreiner, Ramsay MacDonald, Keir Hardie and the Pankhursts. And when one of the most memorable political campaigns in British history was planned and nurtured there, Holmwood found itself in the national spotlight.

The house's owners had begun life as social campaigners. From a liberal middle-class Bristol family Emmeline Pethick had formed the Esperance Club to alleviate the effects of poverty on working-class girls. Born into wealth Frederick Lawrence had become involved in philanthropic work whilst at Cambridge and was treasurer of the Mansfield House project in Canning Town when he met Emmeline who was then working for the West London Mission. She refused his first proposal, fearing that marriage would not allow her to carry on her social and campaigning work, not least because Fred was a prospective Liberal Unionist MP and she a socialist. Converted, he renounced his candidacy and invested in a socialist London paper. During their engagement the couple brought deprived children down to Leith Hill and Friday Street and at their marriage in 1901 MPs mixed with slum dwellers. He had married Emmeline, Fred said, because she smoked, could get off a moving bus, and went walking without gloves. In respect for her desire to keep her own identity, he added her name to his.

The Pethick Lawrences kept an apartment at Clements Inn and took the Dutch House as their country home. Built in 1897 by Wildman Cattley, it was described by Pevsner as *'somewhat outré'* because the rooms radiate in a Y shape from a central hallway. Designed by Lutyens, in 1901 it stood in eight acres. *'If I have ten springs here,'* wrote Emmeline, *'I shall be happy with my lot.'* Others had equally warm feelings; the suffragette Annie Kenney wrote that she had never enjoyed home life as she did when she visited: *'it was a privilege and a deep pleasure.'*

The couple renamed the house the Mascot, added a billiard room, (now Oak Tree House), put in rose gardens and a pond and built sleeping platforms in the trees.

THE GOVERNMENT'S POUND OF FLESH

The Dutch House, then known as the Mascot, in 1912. There have since been alterations to the roof line and the addition of dormer windows whilst development has devoured the garden to north and south.
The figures in the foreground are probably Mrs Pethick Lawrence and her housekeeper, Mai Start.
(Votes for Women courtesy of the British Library Colindale)

The Mascot, Holmwood, the Country House of Mr. and Mrs. Pethick Lawrence
(Where the Government are threatening a sale of the furniture to pay the costs of the recent trial.)

Fred donated a billiard table to the village club, hosted cricket teas and became known locally as 'Great Pethick'. Emmeline hosted fetes where local children were entertained with old English games and fairy scenes performed by the Esperance Club for whom an upper room was set aside. Then, in 1904, they engaged Arnold Dunbar Smith, who had designed the Passmore Edwards Centre in Tavistock Square, to design a separate place of respite for impoverished women and children.

This purposeful country life came to an end in 1906, however, when Emmeline Pethick Lawrence became treasurer of the Women's Social and Political Union.

In 1903 Emmeline Pankhurst had formed the radical Manchester-based WSPU and the publicity grabbing tactics of her daughter, Christabel, had made headlines. The organization needed to be based in London, however, and in 1906 the organizational services of Emmeline Pethick Lawrence were recommended to Mrs Pankhurst by Keir Hardie, leader of the Independent Labour Party. Though she had come to believe in women's suffrage, (reasoning that if women could vote then issues of child poverty would become political, rather than philanthropic issues), Emmeline was not keen to get involved: '*To tell the truth I had no fancy to be drawn into a small group of brave and reckless and quite helpless people who were prepared to dash themselves against the oldest tradition of human civilization as well as one of the strongest governments of modern times,*' she wrote. She was, however, persuaded.

The WSPU set up office in the Pethick Lawrences' Clements Inn apartment. Emmeline organised its finances, spoke at rallies, designed its colours and directed policy.

Meanwhile Fred, with Keir Hardie, paid off the organisation's debts and launched 'Votes for Women'. Described as the most persuasive beggar in London for the amount of money she raised, Emmeline was arrested in October 1906 on attempting to make a speech outside the houses of Parliament. She refused to be bound over to keep the peace and was sentenced to two months in Holloway where she had a breakdown. Fred was mocked in the papers when he pledged £10 to the Union for every day that she remained imprisoned. He responded by taking his wife's place as treasurer, giving legal advice and personally standing bail for those arrested. Becoming known as 'Godfather', he was always ready to stand bail at police stations, said Ethel Smyth, day or night, his money bag at his feet.

Built on the site of a couple of ancient cottages a few hundred yards north of the Mascot, the Sundial had two dormitories and, on the side facing out onto to the Common, a mural on which is painted the inscription: '*Let others tell of storms and showers, I tell of sunny morning hours.*'
A stone laid in the hall reads: '*In Praise of Mother Earth and of her daughter the Green Lady*', in reference to the myth of Demeter and Persephone. (Emmeline had founded a similar hostel named 'the Green Lady' by the sea in Littlehampton.)
At the opening ceremony in 1904 local children knocked at the door to be admitted by a fairy who joined them for dances in the garden.

Mrs Pethick Lawrence, standing, with Emmeline Pankhurst and Annie Kenney, with the Pethick Lawrences' Holmwood driver, Mr Rapley, (who was famed for his discretion about WSPU matters), at the wheel.
(Elizabeth Crawford)

When Christabel Pankhurst arrived in London it was with the Pethick Lawrences that she lived for the next five years and with them she came each weekend to Holmwood. The Daily News dubbed the Mascot the 'unofficial headquarters of the WSPU'. *'It was only at the weekend in my country house that the three of us had enough leisure to thrash out together any complicated problem,'* recalled Fred. Annie Kenney concurred: *'Processions, Albert Hall meetings, raids on Parliament, tactics in prison, the varied forms of advertisement… all were decided, debated, discussed, analysed and counter discussed round the breakfast, lunch and dinner table at the Lawrences' home, in the old courts around the Strand, round the fire at Holmwood or in the woods around Leith Hill. If the beautiful woods there could have spoken, Scotland Yard would have forestalled many a militant action.'* At weekends MPs, labour leaders, suffragette factory girls and titled ladies played and plotted over bowling matches in the garden.

With Christabel's arrival campaigning took a radical turn. Arrest and imprisonment became a publicity strategy and afterwards many recuperated in Holmwood with Emmeline who repeatedly endured prison herself. Just before Christmas 1908 Mrs Pankhurst and Christabel found themselves released late at night to find Clements Inn shut up for the weekend. With nowhere to go they took the train to Holmwood where Christabel recovered with long walks on Leith Hill. Travelling back to London for a belated release parade, they returned to Holmwood for Christmas and New Year.

By 1910 the struggle had grown bitter. In November of that year the police inflicted horrific violence on unarmed women in retaliation for which windows were smashed in London's streets. The Pethick Lawrences may already have been uneasy about the way that

The tree platforms in the garden of the Mascot from which suffragettes would practise their speeches or sleep out on warm nights. The garden, then several acres, looked directly out over Leith Hill.
In his autobiography Fred Pethick Lawrence wrote movingly of his joy at returning to his Holmwood garden after his time in prison.
(Illustration by Elliot Seabrooke from The Surrey Hills by FE Green, published by Chatto & Windus. Reprinted by permission of The Random House Group Ltd.)

Christabel was taking the campaign; there is no evidence of Emmeline having cast a stone or used a hammer, indeed she and Fred later discussed passive resistance with Gandhi. Nor was the violence orchestrated. Nonetheless, as leaders, they were responsible. In May of 1912 they were arrested alongside Mrs Pankhurst and charged with 'conspiracy to incite persons to commit malicious damage.' Their trial became a great spectacle: the papers reported daily on the womens' dress and the flowers that they carried.

'*Beloved,'* wrote Fred to his wife on the eve of the verdict: '*We are very near to a great day, the greatest that we have seen in our lives. To me it seems that an honour such as is conferred only on a few in many centuries is about to be conferred on us. We are to stand where the great and noble have stood before us all down the ages. We are to be linked with those who have won the everlasting homage of the whole human race. If next week you and I were to be crowned King and Queen in the presence of an adulating people, how paltry would be the honour in comparison. It is supreme joy that you and I will stand there together.'*

On giving the guilty verdict the jury told the judge that they unanimously hoped that: '*taking into consideration the undoubtedly pure motives that underlie the agitation'* he would '*be pleased to exercise the utmost clemency and leniency.'* He was not. The defendants were sentenced to nine months, she, together with Mrs Pankhurst, in Holloway, he in Wormwood Scrubs. Both underwent forcible feeding.

The Mascot was left to the care of housekeeper Mai Start who divided her time between London and Holmwood. As part of a campaign of harassment of the authorities she sought constant instructions, complaining to the prison governor that poor Mrs Pethick Lawrence had three establishments to run, to which the exasperated man replied that '*people who have three establishments to run ought to take care not to find themselves in prison.'*

On their release the Pethick Lawrences met with Mrs Pankhurst and Christabel in Boulogne. (Rather than stand trial Christabel had fled to France and was living in Paris). A disagreement ensued, the couple being of the opinion that an escalation in violence would squander the goodwill engendered by the trial. Despite their misgivings at the Pankursts' plans for the forthcoming autumn campaign the couple fully intended to return to their positions within the Union after a period of recuperation. Then, whilst staying with Emmeline's brother in Canada they discovered that the government was seeking to recover the prosecution costs from them under a new sanction aimed at deterring those offering financial assistance to the Union. Mrs Pankhurst urged them to remain in Canada and to remove their assets there.

Though he could have written a cheque for the costs Fred refused to do so. Having staked his health and life in the cause of human equality, he said, he could not renounce it because of the risk to property. '*The warfare between us and the government has now been carried on to the financial plane,'* he wrote, '*and the only course consistent with my principles is to fight every inch of the way. I take identically the same view of the present situation that I took of my personal position when I refused to abandon the hunger strike, though threatened with forcible feeding.'* He did, however, safeguard the Mascot by selling it to Emmeline's brother-in-law, Thomas Mortimer Budgett of Lyme Regis.

The couple returned from Canada to find the Mascot occupied by bailiffs. Their possessions - books, furniture and pictures - were to be auctioned. 'Burglary', Fred dubbed the government's actions in 'Votes for Women'.

The Holmwood Sale

L.N.A.

MR. PETHICK LAWRENCE ADDRESSING THE CROWD

Poster advertising the auction and Mr Pethick Lawrence addressing the crowd in the back garden of the Mascot. *(Votes for Women courtesy of the British Library, Colindale)*

The WSPU launched the 'Holmwood Campaign'. For six weeks from Mid September until the end of October rallies were held at the Norfolk Arms and on the Common. Meetings were held in Ockley, Westcott, and Bookham and every night for weeks in Dorking. Sylvia Pankhurst, Annie Kenney and all those with local connections came down to speak, organizer 'Charlie' Marsh allaying the fears of Dorking tradesmen that the women would go on a window breaking spree with assurances that their only intention was to draw attention to the injustice of the government's action. A huge amount of sympathy was elicited, not to mention donations.

Adverts in the suffragette press urged supporters to attend on the 31st of October. Many came by train in suffragette colours and by one o'clock 3-4000 had gathered. The couple walked up from the Sundial. Fred addressed the crowd, then Emmeline. Many of the couple's possessions were returned to them, purchased, wrote one observer, *'by those who could appreciate the single-mindedness of Mr and Mrs Pethick Lawrence who had risked so much in both health and pocket for the cause they had at heart.'* Even the auctioneer, who had already expressed his appreciation for the courtesy Fred had shown his men, bought an item and returned it to them.

A carved plaque in the hallway of the house quotes Milton: *'O Liberty! Thou choicest treasure! Oct 31 1912',* in commemoration of that day.

The sale marked the end of the Pethick Lawrences' involvement with the WSPU. The Union's offices were moved out of Clements Inn and Mrs Pankhurst issued a statement that as they could not approve militant policy the couple had left the organization. Neither made public their feelings at this betrayal nor did they call upon others to leave, though many did so. There was more to the split than the challenge to Christabel's authority, however. The couple's wealth had become a liability to the organization: in a campaign of property damage concern that Fred would be sued for the consequences of their activities might have inhibited women from acting.

The WSPU embarked upon a campaign of stone throwing and arson. Without the guiding hands of the Pethick Lawrences, however, finances were never again secure, nor public support so assured. The couple continued to campaign through the United Suffragists, opposing the 'Cat and Mouse Act', (a term coined by Fred), but they also found new causes for their energies. During the 1913 labour troubles in Dublin they offered a home at the Sundial to starving children, six of whom attended South Holmwood School.

On the outbreak of war Emmeline brought Belgian refugees to Holmwood through the Women's Emergency Corps. Fred was a founder of the Union of Democratic Control, the leading anti-war movement whilst Emmeline campaigned with the Women's Peace Movement. When conscripted, at the age of forty-six, he refused to serve on the grounds that he was an objector of a political kind. Awarded an exemption as long as he did work of national importance, he was offered labouring work by FE Green, an old comrade who had written for 'Votes for Women', at his smallholding, Baringsfield in Newdigate. The Dorking military tribunal instead sent him to Wattlehurst Farm in Capel.

The Pethick Lawrences on a visit to the United States in the 1920s. *(Library of Congress)*

Both stood unsuccessfully for parliament in 1918. They left Holmwood for Peaslake in 1920 and in 1923 Fred became a Labour MP. He served as Financial Secretary to the Treasury and Secretary of State for India in Attlee's government. Created 1st Baron Lawrence of Peaslake, he remarried after Emmeline's death in 1954. His second wife, Helen Craggs, was a suffragette arsonist for whom he had stood bail forty years earlier. He died in 1961.

The Great War in Holmwood

I n August 1914 Canon Palmes at St Mary Magdalene announced that a bell would toll at twelve each day and asked that those who heard it might lift their hearts to God for the sake of those serving at the front.

The effects of war were immediately felt: horses were commandeered and the bus service reduced. Trees at Redlands were cut for pit-props and trench linings. Mrs Pethick Lawrence took in Belgian refugees at the Sundial, Lord Ashbourne at Moorhurst. Cuthbert Heath gave pep talks to Holmwood volunteers in his office at Anstie and invited the London Civil Service Rifles to drill in his grounds. Meanwhile his London office became a recruitment centre with attesting officers to swear in Lloyds men wanting to join up, as had his own son, Leopold Cuthbert.

'Our family is doing well,' recorded his daughter, Genesta in late 1914, for seven of her eight cousins had enlisted. Cuthbert's brother, Arthur Raymond, involved himself with the Surrey Guides, the Soldiers and Sailors Help Society, the Dorking War Pensions Committee and the special constables. His wife, Flora, trained in massage and worked at Leatherhead Red Cross hospital, later providing convalescence to shell-shocked soldiers at Kitlands. So high ranking were Sir Leopold's heirs - Major General Sir Gerard Moore Heath was Chief Engineer to the 1st army in France - that attempts were made to infiltrate the household. In 1915 a woman purporting to be Danish applied for a job as governess to Genesta. She was jailed as a German spy.

Not everyone, however, was in favour: when Cuthbert Heath arranged a recruitment meeting in August 1914 a drunk heckled. The Pethick Lawrences began campaigning for peace. Nor was Mr Pethick Lawrence the only conscientious objector: EW Turner was offered work of 'national importance' locally by Mr Isemonger, which proposal was rejected by the military tribunal who required him to work at a flour mill in Ewell.

Emmeline Pethick Lawrence (far left) aboard the liner Noordam on her way to The Hague Peace Conference in April 1915 with international delegates. *(Library of Congress)*

Holmwood's farm workers were exempt from military service. Other employers struggled to prevent their staff being called up, making applications to the Military Tribunal on behalf of their butchers, bakers, shop staff, timber fellers and wood workers. Albert Turner of the White Hart tried to hang on to his cab drivers. Colonel Helsham Jones and Cuthbert Heath applied to exempt gardeners, gamekeepers and chauffeurs. Mr Keep of the Hut (Bentleys) sat on the Tribunal and many came before him time and again as they moved jobs or their employment was re-classified. At first conditional exemptions were freely given, but as time went on even those with starred exemptions, like the carrier, John Hoad, were required to serve. And those in vital agricultural work were required to drill with the local militia, unless, like Arthur Piper, the bailiff at Inholms, they were adjudged to have no time in which to do so.

Mrs John Stavridi, nee Anina Olga Valieri on presentation at court in 1911 - from a photograph held by the Victoria and Albert Museum. Mrs Stavridi's husband, John (later Sir John) Stavridi of Ferndale Cottage, played a key diplomatic role during the war. A banker and Greek Consul to London he was sent on a mission to prevent the Greek government holding to a policy of strict neutrality which would have required the Greeks to disarm and intern British and French troops retreating through their territory. This he achieved by negotiation and the threat of a blockade. He then organised the chartering of Greek mercantile marine to the Allies. After the war he was knighted for his services. The Stavridis' daughter, Joanna, was awarded a Distinguished War Certificate during World War Two when she was matron in charge of a Red Cross Hospital in Crete.

Civilians also applied themselves: Mrs Bell of Moor Lodge organised parcels for prisoners of war; others held sewing parties to make clothes for soldiers and schoolchildren knitted with materials supplied by Mrs Habershon of Brook Lodge.

Immediately on the outbreak a defence committee was organised for the Dorking area under the Defence of the Realm Act. A sub-committee had responsibility for the parishes of North and South Holmwood and Coldharbour. Chaired by George Henry Longman of Holmwood Cottage, the Holmwood Defence Committee's first task in November 1914 was to compile a list of all horses, cattle and sheep and of cars and motorcycles so that plans might be made for the evacuation of everything that might be of assistance to the Kaiser's armies should invasion occur.

Assuming that any attack would come from the south 'clearances' were to be driven towards Berkshire and Buckinghamshire. Drovers were appointed to accompany the animals and special constables sworn in to police the evacuation. Animals from the Holmwoods were to progress via Wotton and Abinger, where they would merge with columns from other districts, thence through Clandon, Worplesden, Pirbright, Bisley and Bagshot to Windsor Great Park. (The route was amended in 1915 to go via Stonebridge, Dorking, Ranmore and West Horsley.) Livestock was to have mustered at Anstie Grange and at Holmwood Farm, vehicles at Moorhurst.

Assessments were made as to the number of wagons required to transport fodder, horseshoes, iron, anvils, grindstones and the like that were not to fall into enemy hands. Consideration had also to be given to the needs of the herds that might be passing through from Sussex and Kent, taking the same route thereafter as the Holmwood herds, and for those of the slaughtermen accompanying the animals. There was no general evacuation plan for human residents, however, though a sub-committee was formed comprising the vicars of North and South Holmwood and of Coldharbour, together with a number of local women, to compile lists of mothers with infants, the elderly and infirm who might require to be removed.

In April 1915 Mr Longman had fifteen special constables appointed. By February 1916 another twelve were serving. Soon, however, so many men were in France that he was having difficulty in finding men for driving duty. The list making continued into 1916 – bicycles, firearms, ammunition – though by this time the Committee was encountering resistance to its enquiries. Finally, though, the threat of invasion receded. The special constables were stood down. The war was far from over, however.

It was a time of deprivation. Fuel grew short and holly was allocated for burning. Lady Laura Hampton opened a soup kitchen and the vicar instituted fortnightly gatherings at the village club. Civilian organisations struggled. The Prosecuting Society's annual dinner was cancelled in 1915, never to be re-established. Maggie Worrow took on the role of treasurer to the Foresters as well as running the Norfolk when her husband was called up. Mr Lay left South Holmwood School to join the services. A woman, Frances Morris, acted as his emergency replacement until Stephen Bowring was appointed temporary headmaster at the end of 1914. By December of the following year he had been accepted for the army, despite having been rejected on four occasions because of his defective eyesight and an application by the school board to the military tribunal for exemption. On the day of her arrival in March 1916 his replacement, Lucy Strudwick, sent the children home for lack of teachers. Many of the older pupils had already been exempted from attendance to undertake farm work. It was with difficulty that the school operated at all in the face of pupils taken out, low attendance, staff sickness and resignations. Canon Palmes struggled all winter to keep it running despite a lack of coke to run the stoves but was defeated in 1917 by measles and diphtheria epidemics, each of which had the school shut for a month. By early 1918 numbers were at an all-time low: only twenty-one children out of 135 were in attendance on one day in January, before the school closed again for a whooping cough epidemic.

Arthur Raymond Heath of Kitlands, previously MP for Louth in Lincolnshire and the least distinguished of Sir Leopold's sons, lost his son, Raymond Leopold Grieg Heath in 1915. He was killed by a sniper and is commemorated in a memorial window at Coldharbour depicting troops in battle dress.

The voluntary fire brigade also struggled: at the outbreak thirteen volunteers were sworn in as special constables and employed guarding railway bridges; others joined the services. In 1916, with only one fireman available, applications were made for exemption from military service for Chief Fire Officer Secretan and engineers Mercer and Worsfold. On refusal a reserve brigade of men over military age or exempt was formed.

In 1916 the horrors of war were brought into the heart of the Holmwood when Cuthbert Heath offered Anstie Grange for use as a hospital for officers, fitting it out at his own expense. Casualties were brought into Holmwood by train. At the station they were decanted onto ambulances and driven to Anstie in convoy, often late at night. In February 1917 an unexpected patient arrived on one of these convoys, Frederick Dunbar Heath, son of Arthur Raymond and Flora. (His brother had already been killed.) Though his parents were barred from Anstie, Caroline Heath lifted her prohibition to allow them to walk over daily to see their son.

On November 11th 1918 the telephone rang all day at Anstie. A dance was hastily arranged, though there was but one man with whom to dance.

The memorial brass set into a pew at St John the Evangelist to Hugo Molesworth Legge of Holmwood Lodge who was killed in action in 1915 aged 24. His mother, Cordelia Molesworth Twysden Legge is buried at South Holmwood. Another of her sons, Montague George Bentinck Legge DSO (later Rear Admiral) captained HMS Nerissa at the Battle of Jutland.

Returning soldiers found the Holmwoods changed: with shortages of man-power, draught animals and fuel, farmers had struggled. The grand houses had lost their staff, (at Anstie the internal domestic staff was cut from sixteen to three), their gardens and greenhouses planted with necessities. Even after the end of hostilities food remained scarce. And illness continued: at South Holmwood there were so many children absent in November of 1918 that the medical officer closed the school for two weeks.

The sons of master and servant had served and died. Sydney Hack of the Knoll lost his son, Adrian. The Habershons of Brook Lodge lost Philip and Sidney; Hugo Molesworth Legge of Holmwood Lodge was killed, whilst the Heaths lost Raymond Leopold Grieg Heath and Martin Heath Caldwell, (grandson of Sir Leopold and of Colonel Helsham Jones).

In 1920 it was proposed that the dead of Holmwood be included on Dorking's war memorial. At South Holmwood, however, a committee raised funds for a separate memorial designed by Sir Montague Omanay of Redlands. Late in the day the committee were asked to include the name of Victor Tickner of Brook House, who had died of septic pneumonia in 1916 whilst serving in the Navy. He had cut his throat in a fit of insanity. His inclusion was unanimously agreed. Standing at the roadside, the memorial to the twenty-seven men of South Holmwood was dedicated on October 9th 1921. A commemorative tablet, (incorporating three additional names), was placed in St Mary Magdalene and framed copies were presented to the next-of-kin by local boy-scouts. A roll of honour was placed in the village club and in 1922 the school unveiled its own memorial. A further seventeen lives are commemorated at St John's and on Dorking's memorial.

Anstie Grange Military Hospital

Nearly 700 patients passed through Anstie Grange. The flag that flew over the hospital was later given to Genesta Heath (Hamilton): it now hangs in Coldharbour church. Living from time to time in and around Holmwood, Genesta, who had a farm in Kenya, bought Scammels Corner in 1969. Her memoir, 'A Stones Throw', recounts times at Anstie before and during the war when she acted as pantry maid at the hospital. Cuthbert Heath was presented with a certificate for display at Anstie in 1920 in acknowledgement of the Army Council's gratitude. He also received an OBE. *(Dorking Museum)*

MrVanderbilt, the Holmwood and the Lusitania

'In memory of Alfred Gwynne Vanderbilt
A gallant gentleman and fine sportsman who perished in the Lusitania May 7th 1915.
This stone erected on his favourite road by a few of his British coaching friends and admirers.'

Multi-millionaire scion of the American banking and railroad family, Alfred Gwynne Vanderbilt spent as much time in Britain as the United States. Horses were his passion and he often raced carriages from the South Coast to London, recreating the great days of private coach travel. On reaching Holmwood his coachman, attired in a gold-braided coat and top hat, would blow his horn to bring out local children in the hope of pennies or sweets.

In 1912 Vanderbilt was married in Reigate, (for a second time, his first wife having divorced him for adultery with the wife of the Cuban Ambassador to London), to Margaret Emerson McKim, then living in Betchworth.

In 1915 Alfred Vanderbilt left New York on the Lusitania, despite German warnings that British ships in Atlantic waters should consider themselves at risk of attack. On the seventh day of the voyage the ship was sunk by a torpedo. Thirty-eight when he died, Vanderbilt left a son by his first wife and two infants by his second. His roadside memorial, on the northbound carriageway between South and Mid Holmwood, was erected by his friends from the British Horse Society. A small fund provides for its maintenance. *(Photograph Library of Congress)*

Where the country began

Between the wars the world poured into the Holmwood every summer. The public houses accommodated coach-loads for tea, ice-cream and beer. The village club, the Well refreshment rooms at the old chapel, Tollgate Cottage, Cyprus Villa and North Holmwood's roadside shops all served teas. In 1930 sales particulars for the Elms near the Norfolk noted its *'exceptional facilities... for running as a café or refreshment house'*. It became the Bell Holm Hotel. The Norfolk too began to go by the grander title of 'Hotel'. Small houses were rented weekly. Larger ones were advertised in the national press and let for whole summers. Even so, it was often impossible to meet demand.

Though many came by rail, petrol was the future. Holmwood's roadside businesses soon adapted: at Fernhurst John Hoad begun repairing vehicles as an adjunct to his carrying business, selling petrol by the can. The business evolved into the Holmwood Garage. A similar metamorphosis took place at the Norfolk where Eric Pierce installed petrol pumps on Isemonger's pond in the early 1920s, profiting from the passing motor trade as had his grandfather from horse and carriage. Not that road travel was necessarily reliable: Miss Mitchell had constantly to cancel her cookery lessons at South Holmwood School because of bus breakdowns and the *'bad state of the road'*. Nor was traffic congestion slow in coming: by the 1920s the geese for which the Norfolk was renowned frequently caused tailbacks as they wandered onto the road. As early as 1921 Mr Pethick Lawrence cited traffic as one of his reasons for leaving Holmwood and by 1929 it had been suggested that a London to Brighton road might be driven through the villages. With such proposals, and with the spread of Dorking's suburbs southwards and the expansion of the brickworks, Holmwood's tranquillity was under threat.

The era of the great estates was coming to an end. In 1914 Augustus Perkins sold the house at Oakdene, (together with Vigo), to Henrietta Keswick. On the retained land he built Brookwood, a more modest mansion. In 1929 the executors of John Bruce Nichols auctioned Holmwood Park in lots. The sales particulars acknowledge the lack of demand for servant-dependent mansions with labour-intensive grounds in these difficult times, suggesting that Grandon Lodge's fifteen bed and dressing rooms might make a school or guest house. Similarly, on the death of the last of George Gough's children in 1919 the 'commodious residence' at Wymbletons was offered separately from Fourwents Cottage and the farm buildings providing an *'eligible building site'* with *'ample space for the formation of a carriage drive'*. And in 1922 the

Run by the Misses Jackson and Milne, the Beehive near the station served tea and sold home-produced honey, advertising *'country produce for the flat in town'* to those returning to the station. *(Dorking Museum)*

Stilwell banking family separated the 'residential estate' and 'pleasure farm' at Folly Farm from Bushey Croft Cottages with a view to freeing up '*several fine building sites*' for development. Any property with a piece of agricultural land or a sizable garden was marketed for its building potential, though by no means all of these proposals came to fruition in these difficult financial times.

Augustus Perkins' new residence at Brookwood situated on part of the Oakdene estate from which its grounds were taken. The Perkins were in the brewing business with the Barclays of Bury Hill. On Perkins' death in 1921 the estate was split again. It is probably no coincidence that the house was acquired by another brewer, Bertram Watney. *(Dorking Museum)*

If the estates in the heart of the Holmwood were dissolving, those on the Common's northern periphery were more vulnerable still. There, where there was increasing industry and a demand for lower cost housing a large garden might be split into not just one or two substantial villas but into a score of plots. The grounds of the nearby Deepdene, (sold by Lord Francis Hope, the Duke of Newcastle[19], to the Metropolitan Railway in 1921), were developed for small scale housing within walking distance of Dorking and the station in the 1920s. A tide of smaller houses was sweeping south from Dorking,

Known in the mid-17th century as Maryfields and as Whitehouse Farm when part of the Bury Hill estate, Folly Farm acquired a grand stone house in the 18th century. On the break up of the Bury Hill estate it was acquired by the Duke of Norfolk and was tenanted by the Bowring family for most of the 19th century at the end of which it was acquired by the Stilwell banking family and let to Walter Barker, the Holmwood butcher. *(Dorking Museum)*

---

[19] He had inherited the title through his father and the Deepdene through his mother, taking the Hope name. Short of cash, the Duke had let the house since the turn of the century. After the sale it became a grand hotel.

making the mansions to the north of the Common less desirable. They also sat uncomfortably close to the brickworks and in 1936 Bentsbrook, a small house by local standards at only seven bedrooms and 18 acres, fell victim to these pressures. Marketed as a building estate, *'ripe for [the] immediate development of shops and small houses'*, Boehm's mansion made way for an estate of detached houses.

Industrial North Holmwood – the brickworks

On the corner of Spook Hill and Holmesdale Road the Dorking Brick Company's offices were refaced and extended in 1931 as a showcase. Between two stations, the site was a small operation until the 1920s when production expanded westwards across Stubs Farm and the workforce grew to sixty or seventy. The bricks produced there, (which moved across the site by a two foot gauge steam railway), were used all over the south-east, notably in the construction of the Middlesex, Barts and Surrey County hospitals. The Company ran another site at Beare Green and in 1935 merged with the Sussex Brick Company. *(Dorking Museum)*

Workers at the brickyard in the 1930s. *(Dorking Museum)*

North Holmwood-based Harry Leggett (2nd left) and his steam lorry at the brickworks in the 1920s with Percy Skilton, Alf Knight and Stan Racey who was found drowned in a London dock. *(Dorking Museum)*

By the interwar period the freeholds to many farms had been sold and copyholds enfranchised. Ownership of the Manor was not nearly as valuable as in centuries past when rents, quit rents and fines had brought in a steady income. Now the Common generated paltry sums from the sale of timber, holly and wayleaves. It was a liability, not least because of the constant wrangling with the Committee that struggled to prevent it becoming an overgrown morass. In 1921 the Duke of Norfolk sought to dispose of what remained of the Manor. Though Cuthbert Heath bought the Duke's Warren on Leith Hill, Redlands Wood attracted derisory offers. The remaining freeholds together with the Common and roadside wastes, sporting rights and the entitlement to rents and fines failed to reach its reserve. Manor and Common remained the responsibility of the Duchy. In 1925 the Law of Property Acts converted all remaining copyholds to freeholds, so depriving the Duchy even of its quit rents. By the 1930s visitors probably thought that the Common was publicly owned for a spate of beauty spots had been given to local authorities including the Glory Woods (by the Duke of Newcastle in 1929) and the Nower (by Lt Col Barclay in 1931). Holmwood Common, however, remained commonly grazed and publicly enjoyed, but privately owned.

For locals it remained a resource. The ladies of the Beehive kept hives there. Others made fruit syrups, or, like Pedlar Barnes and William Bacon, collected florists' moss, or made brooms or faggots, ferreted for rabbits or cut holly for wreaths. Many kept livestock there into the 1930s and the ancient custom of bracken-cutting continued into the century.

Good times return to Capel Lyse and Anstie Grange

Kathleen Keswick (left) on presentation at court in 1923 – from a photograph held by the Victoria and Albert Museum. Kathleen was the daughter of the MP for Epsom, William Keswick of the Jardines shipping family, and his wife, Henrietta, whom he had married when he was 64 and she 24. An international hockey player, a trained singer and one of the first women in Britain to hold a driving licence, Henrietta Keswick (nee Barrington) bought the house at Oakdene and part of the estate on being widowed, renaming it Capel Lyse. There she lived with her two daughters by Keswick and her second husband. Cyril Cameron Pyke, who had had a colourful colonial career in the Far East and Africa, collecting medals from Belgium, Rumania and Serbia in addition to his OBE. At Capel Lyse he farmed black pigs whilst she became president of the WI, known for her fetes and for opening her gardens for charity.

At Anstie Grange Cuthbert Heath (right) entertained, hunting with the Surrey Union hounds or shooting in Redlands Wood when he was not in London, the south of France or on his yacht, the Anne of Anstie. In 1921 he bought the 200 acre Duke's

Warren on Leith Hill from the Duke of Norfolk, donating it in 1933 to the National Trust. He had paid little for it at a time when such landscapes were more common and less prized, he reasoned, and by giving it away he could ensure that it was not sold for development to pay taxes on his death. *'It will give enormous pleasure to lots of people for ever, I hope,'* he said. He also acquired Redlands Wood when it was threatened with development and opened up paths through it. On his death in 1939 tenants, servants and farm labourers filed past his coffin.
(JJ Heath Caldwell)

By the 1930s the Cabin at North Holmwood was selling tobacco, confectionery, newspapers and general provisions. It had also taken over the sub-post office from Frost's next door and become a telephone call office. *(Dorking Museum)*

Though the days of local food supplies were over locals did not have far to go for their daily needs: the Crofts now had competition from two bakers; the Bucklands had progressed via market gardening to competing in the fruit trade with Payne's; Hamlin's in Warwick Road provided a grocery, Stanford's a general store and Smith's a news agency. The village boasted sweeps, cobblers, decorators, timber merchants and a firewood dealer, not to mention the cottage tailors, dressmakers and laundresses. It was also served by various roundsmen bringing fish and chips, winkles, ice-cream and muffins.

The self-sufficiency of the Holmwoods was diminishing, however, as local government expanded[20]. In 1930 the voluntary fire brigade found itself redundant when the Rural and Urban District councils jointly formed a brigade for the whole Dorking area. There came an end to drill nights, to church parades and the annual sports day. (The Crofts next door took over the shed and yard.) Likewise the Foresters' importance was undermined by the development of the welfare state. By the 1920s there was a safety net for the working classes in hard times and a state pension. The last church parade was held in 1928 though turnouts had been falling even before that. Stalwarts Walter Pierce and Harry Isemonger both died in 1935, and, though Pierce's sons took over, the organisation never again played so large a role in the social and economic life of the Holmwood.

The Voluntary Fire Brigade's final drill night. In the background are Steyning Cottage, Crofts' bakery and post office, and the fire station. The boys in caps are the callboys. Mr Secretan had been followed as chief officer by Norman Beyfus of Daisy Lodge then by William Kingham of Brook Lodge. From the mid 1920s the brigade found it difficult to obtain horses and, with Albert Hoad's lorry often unavailable to pull the pump, a motorised engine was bought in 1927 by public subscription. With the establishment of the Dorking brigade, however, the Holmwood men stood down and the brigade held its farewell dinner on 9th April 1930. *(Dorking Museum)*

---

[20] From 1933 North Holmwood fell into Dorking Urban District for local government purposes and the rest of the Holmwood into Dorking and Horley Rural District

South Holmwood Scout Troop was founded by Captain Ayrton of the Church Army in 1911 and later lead by headmasters. *(Des Scutt)*

Local schools, however, remained at the centre of children's lives. At South Holmwood Arthur Lay returned from the war in 1919 only to resign four months later. His replacement, Mr Williams, established a football club and a girls' badminton team and inaugurated the first sports day in 1925. He also ran the scout troop, arranging for the Priory Cottage mission room from Mid Holmwood to be re-erected in the school grounds. Their female counterparts used the school premises at North Holmwood until a headquarters was built in the garden of Holm Cottage.

If the children's social lives were centred around the schools, adult social activity was centred around the inns and the village club. The green opposite the Holly and Laurel hosted the fire brigade, scout and Sunday school sports days. The 'Comrades of the Great War', played football matches behind the White Hart. The South Holmwood Old Boys fielded a team, as did the brickworks. There were billiards and stool ball teams and an annual five mile race from the Holly and Laurel and back via Four Wents and Inholms. There were midweek cricket fixtures against Metropolitan Police divisions and South London railway teams and in the 1930s games began to be played on a Sunday. At North Holmwood, where for many years the game had been played behind the church, the Duke of Newcastle provided a pitch in 1928 and two teams were fielded every Saturday with Sunday cricket introduced in 1939. The ground provided a recreation area for the village and when the pavilion was constructed with money raised by subscription it became a social centre, dances in the winter months raising funds for the season to come.

A branch of the British Legion was formed in 1921. The Women's Institute, with Canon Palmes in the chair and Mrs Pyke as president, was established the same year. By 1925 it had more than 200 members.

North Holmwood schoolchildren in 1925 *(Des Scutt)*

North Holmwood Sports Club v Morrish Grant & Co, the firm of Mr Morrish of Holmwood Lodge, in the 1930s. *(Des Scutt)*

On the death of landlord Charles Field Pierce his son Walter Jezard Pierce (above) took over his building and undertaking business. Resident at Keston in Mid Holmwood, his 41 years as secretary of the Holmwood Foresters (between 1886 and 1927) was commemorated in 1934 at a smoking concert held in celebration of the organisation's centenary. He also served on the Rural District Council, the parish council and was a charitable trustee. He died in 1936.

Various younger members of the Pierce family continued to be active in the Foresters until its demise in the early 1970s. *(Dorking Advertiser)*

The people of the Holmwoods were participating fully in the organisations of national life, and they celebrated events of national importance with enthusiasm. In 1937 a carnival parade with a carnival queen was held for the coronation of George VI. There were prizes for fancy dress and for the best decorated pram, bicycle and car. Bands competed to play 'A bicycle made for two' outside Mrs Hoad's garage whilst Mrs Ainslie of Moor Lodge, (the school's 'fairy godmother'), donated commemorative mugs.

Travel and contact with new ideas, however, were changing the people of the Holmwoods. The war had returned men to the villages less willing to bow to the wishes of their elders and social betters. The result was something of a crisis at South Holmwood village club in 1920 when the ex-soldiers' football team, the 'Comrades of the Great War', requested that alcohol be served. As the club had been built on land donated by the late Reverend Wickham the Reverend's son, who was living in Somerset, had more say in the running of their club than the people of Holmwood. He agreed that a 'wet canteen' would be acceptable if it was not run for profit. Others in the local community felt it incumbent upon them to protect the morality of the lower orders: Anne Garrett of Holm Cottage referred the matter to her solicitor, claiming that *many who would shrink from going to a public house will have no scruples in drinking at the Hall, the fact that the authorities permit drink there will make it appear quite natural and right.* It would *be leading the young of both sexes into temptation.*

For all this social activity, life in the villages was not easy for many. The vicarage ran a coal and clothing club and those looking for work would walk into Dorking rather than expend 2d on the bus fare. With much accommodation tied to farms or to work at the great houses where staff were housed in attics, gardeners' cottages and stable-lofts there was little to rent, a problem that the Rural District Council proposed to address in 1919 with the building of twenty-four low-rent cottages. Even at the proposed rents of 12/6d per week, however, they were out of the reach of many.

Petrol pumps at the Norfolk Garage. *(Dorking Museum)*

In 1927 one of the first by-passes in Britain was constructed around Dorking. Cutting through what was left of the Deepdene to meet the Horsham road at North Holmwood it channelled traffic through the Holmwood. So much had traffic increased by the early 1930s that insurance against damage to passing motorists was necessary at the pitch by the Holly and Laurel and a net had to be erected along the roadside. In 1937 Horace Dewdney was fatally injured by a car near his home at Sefton Villas and in February of 1938 Miss Dixon was thrown off her bicycle outside South Holmwood School. Shortly after that the headmaster warned pupils not to lend cycles to one another after a girl was badly hurt in an accident and a few months later the caretaker was knocked down by a motorbike. If the danger was not enough, by the late 1930s traffic was at a standstill from Dorking to beyond Holmwood Station at weekends and in the evening rush.

The coming war, with its rationing and restrictions, might temporarily relieve the situation but it would only postpone the day when the traffic situation must be dealt with.

Mystery death on the Common

In December 1929 a chauffeur from Redlands Bank Cottages discovered a skeleton on the Common in a makeshift bracken shelter. So decomposed was the body that it was estimated to have been there six months. The man's clothing was of good quality from London stores and empty champagne bottles were found nearby. The body was ascertained to be that of John Morris, a 55 year old commercial clerk from Clapham, who had served in the merchant navy and in the army. Previously employed at the War Office, he appeared to have an independent income. Estranged from his family, he had told his landlady that he was 'dead to everyone' before he disappeared. The cause of death was never discovered, nor what he was doing on the Common.

Carriers in the Holmwood – the Hoad family

In the early 20th century John William Hoad undertook the 11-hour trip to the Spur Inn at Borough and back four times a week in his horse-drawn delivery cart. He also did furniture removals and delivered coal from the station yard. Competition came from Jack Buckland's and from Brown's at the station.
After his death in 1923 his son, Arthur, (above), carried on the business. On moving to Warwick Road, Arthur concentrated on coal deliveries, introducing motor lorries. Other family members also went into the business, notably John Hoad, who established what became the Holmwood Garage. *(Dorking Advertiser)*

Hunting the Holmwood

Cuthbert Heath (left) and his daughter, Genesta (far right) at a hunt meet outside Anstie Grange. Heath had kept the Surrey Union Hunt going during the war years, regularly contributing £500 to funds. In 1919 he became joint master with Henry Lee Steere of Jayes Park who kennelled the hounds. Under Heath's stewardship the hunt met at the Holly and Laurel and at Four Wents. Its committee, of which Mr Bristow Bovill who rented Minnickwood from the Kitlands estate was for 23 years secretary, met at the inn. When in Holmwood the hunt ranged over the Common and the surrounding farms, keeping down the predator that otherwise plagued local smallholders and householders. When the hunt went over the railway line south of Holmwood drivers would often stop to allow riders to pass, a courtesy that came to an end in 1937 with electrification and fencing of the line. The last meet of the Surrey Union Hunt until after the Second World War took place on Holmwood Common on 30th March 1940. Afterwards the dogs were shot. Food was too scarce to justify keeping them. The hunt also lost Major Bovill, killed in action. *(Dorking Museum)*

Hunting with horses was expensive, requiring kennelling for the pack and wages for hunt staff. Only the wealthy participated and even then the Surrey Union was often in dire financial straights. Working men had their own hunt. Here they are meeting outside the Plough at Blackbrook. *(Eileen Fox)*

Home Front in the Holmwood

John Langdon Davies and the Spanish Civil War

John Langdon Davies bought the Sundial from the Pethick Lawrences in 1920. Whilst covering the Spanish Civil War as a journalist he witnessed huge numbers of refugees passing through Santander, many of them children. One of these he found with a note pinned to him saying: *'This is Jose. I am his father. When Santander falls I shall be shot, whoever finds my son, take care of him for me.'* In order to care for and educate such children Langdon Davies, with Eric Muggeridge, established 'Foster Parents Plan for Children in Spain', which extended its reach to the rest of Europe in the 1940s. Plan now works in 45 countries. A prolific political writer, Langdon Davies created the Jackdaw history series for children, wrote on Spain, politics and history and during the Second World War was commander of the South Eastern command Fieldcraft School, writing the 'Homeguard Fieldcraft Manual' and 'Homeguard Warfare' for which he received the MBE. When he was away the Sundial was let for the summers. The above picture shows Langdon Davies with his two young sons in the 1950s. *(Patricia Langdon Davies)*

olmwood had been preparing for more than three years when war was declared in September 1939. An Air Raid Precaution Committee had been formed and the Foresters had announced that they would accept liability for the benefits of any member who was called up even if they had not paid their contributions. Nor was the Holmwood as remote from events in Europe as it might have seemed: a number of refugees from Nazi oppression had found refuge in the vicinity. Former women's magazine journalist, Erika Schmidt-Landry, was living at Ross Cottage with her three small children, trying to earn an income as a toy-maker, whilst Sophie Müller was working as a cook at Minnickwood.

On the first of September the start of term was delayed as South Holmwood School opened as a receiving centre for evacuees. From Dorking station the children were taken by bus to Dorking Halls where they were given a medical examination and a paper bag containing rations for 48 hours – condensed milk, tinned beef, biscuits and chocolate. The first party of thirty boys, ten girls and six adults arrived from Adamsrill Road London County Council School in Sydenham with their teacher, Mr Doswell. His family was billeted with the headmaster, Mr Jay. The next day thirty girls and three of their brothers arrived from Sydenham County Girls School, accompanied by Miss Hartnell, followed by thirty mothers with small children. On the fourth the children were inspected. Some were infested with lice: *'disgusting – you have my sympathy'* wrote the chairman of managers. But the evacuees also had complaints: one girl was billeted with a woman of eighty. The following day the press came to take photographs to accompany reassuring pieces which appeared in the Telegraph and Daily Mail.

The national dailies pictured evacuee children 'somewhere in Surrey'. No indication was given as to where the photographs were taken.

With 119 local children and ninety evacuees, official and 'unofficial', the school was overwhelmed. For the first days the London children were taken for nature walks, but once the woodwork room was filled with trestle tables and the scout mission room drafted in as a classroom lessons recommenced on the eleventh. At North Holmwood, where children had arrived from Grove Vale School, East Dulwich, a solution to the overcrowding was found by working a shift system. Evacuated children and their teachers occupied the school during the morning with off-site activities in the afternoon when local children and 'unofficials' took lessons. After adjustments the school log reports local and evacuee children mixing happily.

At South Holmwood, however, the head of Adamsrill expressed disappointment on finding that his children were taking lessons with the locals though Mr Doswell could hardly take classes for the mixed age ranges present in Holmwood alone, even should a site be found. The London children had to integrate, though their headmaster expressed the wish that *as far as possible [they] should preserve their own identity.'* The problem was never solved and at the end of October the Adamsrill children were transferred to Redhill, (though a number had already returned home when the anticipated bombing campaign had not materialised). Nonetheless the Holmwood had made a favourable impression: *'I didn't know a holiday in the country could be so lovely. I shall always remember it,'* wrote one boy.

Those who remained, (and there was still concern at overcrowding in December though only thirty-seven evacuees remained), found their school hours cut so that the caretaker could complete his evening's work before the blackout. This also enabled the children to get home before darkness, the necessity of which must have been apparent for it was only a few days into the war that Holmwood suffered its first blackout fatality. On a moonless night Stephen Moore, a deaf and elderly gardener from Oakdale Lodge, was fatally injured by a van outside the Holly and Laurel. Not long afterwards George Fairbrother, a labourer from Spring Cottages, fell down some steps in Dorking in the blackout, suffering head injuries. On his death the inquest heard that his mental degeneration had been as a result of that accident in the early weeks of the war.

23RD NOVEMBER 1908   1ST OCTOBER 1939
TO THE MEMORY OF PILOT OFFICER
JOHN C. MACKENZIE HANBURY AUXILIARY AIR FORCE
COUNTY OF SURREY SQUADRON KILLED NEAR THIS
SPOT WHILE ON ACTIVE SERVICE.

A plaque at the Weald School commemorates the pilot whose Gloster Gladiator flew into the ground there whilst on night patrol from Croydon.

Holmwood's German refugees now found themselves 'enemy aliens'. Erika Schmidt-Landry made plans through the Dorking Refugee Committee for her children to go into a Dr Barnardo's home should she be interned. In the event she was not deemed a risk, the Home Office tribunal concluding that she had *formed ties of sympathy with this country'*. When her husband was interned Ralph Vaughan-Williams and EM Forster took up his case. Meanwhile Frau Landry left the Holmwood when she found work as a teacher in a Dr Barnardo's home. Sophie Muller, too, was allowed to remain at liberty. They were not the only ones under suspicion, however. The son of the ex-leader of the briefly independent Ukraine, Pavlo Skoropadsky, was staying with Caroline Heath at Anstie Grange. As Skoropadsky senior was resident in Germany, his son was considered to be of questionable sympathies, and of sufficient concern for military intelligence to vet visitors to Anstie.

Throughout the 'phoney war' preparations were made for the possibility of attack. The school windows were pasted with strip paper. A YMCA canteen was set up at South Holmwood village club. A cohort of the Auxiliary Fire Service was formed and the Foresters resolved that any member whose death was occasioned by the war should have his or her funeral benefits paid.

Everything was requisitioned: time, land and accommodation. The Dutch House became an officers' mess, the Knoll a hospital, and Anstie Grange an officers' training centre and then the headquarters of Queen Alexandra's Imperial Military Nursing Service. Soldiers were billeted at the Norfolk Arms; Canadians occupied Holmwood Park. Even the Scout hut was requisitioned. Gardens and grounds were given over to food production. The manufacturer, Mr Heyman, turned Redlands over to 1500 poultry, likewise Mr Kingham of Brook Lodge who took on 350 chickens. Many, like Miss Beeforth, a school mistress, and Mr Crowther, a Dorking solicitor, who took on the tenancy at Minnickfold in 1942, had little experience and attracted low ratings from Ministry of Food inspectors. Even children's efforts were harnessed: they planted potatoes and collected aluminium and silver foil. Nor was any nutrient left to waste: committees dealt with the collection of waste material and harvested fire-wood from the Common; rose hips were collected from gardens, conkers and foxgloves sent to factories, herbs and nettles harvested and bundled. The headmaster's wife had girls from South Holmwood School making jam from blackberries, plums and elderberries whilst the Women's Institute organised fruit bottling.

Heavy detonations were heard when, in May 1940, the Germans overran France. With invasion feared imminent local children were told not to leave early for school. Names were removed from signposts, the word 'Holmwood' chipped from the stone outside the school.

As the school holidays began rotas were put in place for the daytime care of evacuee children. All such

Holmwood's Auxiliary Fire Service, ladder attached to the roof of their civilian car. *(Dorking Museum)*

routines were severely disrupted throughout August, however, as the Royal Air Force and the Luftwaffe fought for control of the skies above. Holmwood was on the flight path to London and the Royal Observer Corps were stationed on the Common - in a dugout on the football pitch - observing the direction of incoming aircraft. Home guard observers were stationed at North Holmwood where the sports club provided them with shelter. On August 30th the children at South Holmwood were ordered under their desks as a spitfire passed over and crashed to the south-east. A propeller and engine parts fell on the path between Vigo and Capel Lyse, a German instrument was found at the school door and tracer bullets in the gangway. Whenever a plane came down local children would race the police sergeant to the scene on bicycles, despite having been warned not to approach aircraft, unexploded bombs, or parachutes.

Bombing raids on London continued nightly throughout August and September, often lasting from nine in the evening until four in the morning. On the sounding of the sirens some slept out for fear of being killed in their falling houses; others had Anderson shelters dug into their gardens but these filled with water in the clay, becoming uninhabitable if they were not pumped out. School attendance was low, children being without sleep night after night as they listened to the planes going over and heard them returning, jettisoning unused bombs as they went. In mid-August one of these landed at Moorfield, a splinter of it being brought into school by evacuee Roy Golden. A second fell to the rear of Bentsbrook Cottages and Potkiln Cottages, damaging properties nearby. Another fell on Inholms farmland, followed by two more which hit the edge of the brickworks. If farm stock was injured in these blasts, Bert Mann, the slaughterman from Barker's, would be called.

In early September parents refused to allow their children to attend South Holmwood School for fear that troop lorries parked outside might make it a military target. Though the council surveyor found the headmaster's request for an air raid shelter reasonable all that could be offered was glass protection. Parents were presumably not reassured by ongoing battles, nor by the collision of a Hurricane with a Heinkel close by the village. The Hurricane came down in a nearby field, the German plane at Swires Farm in Henfold Lane, three of its crew dying instantly when the plane burst into flames. When its bomb load exploded windows were broken all around and three Auxiliary Fire Service crews were needed to put out the blaze. This was followed by the downing of a Junkers bomber by a Canadian plane. In that incident the crew baled out and children watched as three parachutes opened over the Common, one of the crew landing at Scammels Farm at Blackbrook, another at the Norfolk Arms and a third on Inholms land to the rear of Brookmeadow and Holmwood House. A fourth fell from his harness and was killed on impact, his parachute falling on Holmwood Park. The plane itself came down in the orchard of Folly Farm, narrowly missing the house and causing a Holmwood mother to go into premature labour. The baby died. Then, in early October,

Holmwood Home Guard at Four Wents Pond *(Dorking Museum)*

Holmwood Park was engulfed in fire from an incendiary on a night when bombing continued from dusk until five in the morning.

Eventual success in the Battle of Britain brought an end to the threat of invasion. Aerial activity continued, however, and so frequent were raids on London during October 1940 and so hazardous the children's journeys to school that hours were cut back to nine until one-thirty. It was not until 1941 that the school got its air raid shelters. One benefit of the war however, was the introduction, in October 1942, of lunchtime meals. (They had been provided at North Holmwood since 1937 when Angelus Beyfus left money for the purpose). Served in the woodwork room the first meal was stewed steak, gravy, potatoes and carrots, jam tart and custard.

Captain Henry George Bacon Pinkney DSO MBE MN retired to Sunnyside (Posterns Court) in 1953. In 1941 and 1942 he had played a major part in 'Operation Pedestal', supplying the besieged island of Malta. Setting off in July 1941 as part of a convoy, the Merchant Ship Port Chalmers, of which Pinkney was first officer, was attacked on both arrival and departure. Pinkney was awarded an MBE on his return. A year later Pinkney, who had assumed command of the ship, set off again in a convoy of fourteen ships with a battleship escort. Though bombed south of Sicily, the Port Chalmers was one of only five merchantmen to reach its destination and the only one to do so without suffering damage or casualties. Captain Pinkney received the DSO and was congratulated by secret telegram on the 'gallant and superb seamanship' which had brought his ship to Malta 'in the face of all the enemy could do to prevent it'. (Dorking Museum)

With so many more buildings in use to accommodate evacuees and troops coal supplies ran low. In the winter of 1940/1 closure of the school at South Holmwood was only averted by boys cutting holly on the Common. It was a privilege that the Duke of Norfolk also extended to the Refugee Committee for their hostel in Dorking. Then, in 1943 shortages in rubber and petrol lead to the curtailment of bus services. Labour, too, was in short supply. The school could not replace its caretaker nor could the Common Committee maintain paths and rides. Litter remained uncollected on the cricket pitch and at Four Wents. The lack of labour was compounded by the fact that those not conscripted into the services were serving in the home guard or the auxiliary fire service. Mr Jay often acted as a fire guard all night before returning to school in the morning. The stresses were obvious: he was in a permanently argumentative state by the later stages of the war, barring spectators from school sports day and falling out with parents, staff and vicar.

Even those of other nationalities were required to contribute. Charles Bryant, a neutral Irishman, of 3 Ashleigh Cottages, was imprisoned for 4 months on failing to turn up for home guard duty. The elderly and the very young played their part: in 1944 Miss Hunt of Lothian Cottage, North Holmwood, (sister of the vicar of St Martins and daughter of John Mortimer Hunt of Bellevue - later Holmwood House), died on her way to her Red Cross first aid post duty at the age of 72. Children tended vegetable gardens; the girls at South Holmwood made balaclavas, scarves and socks for ex-pupils in the services; they held bring-and-buy sales to provide aid to the Soviet Union, (about which new ally films were shown in the village club); they fundraised for warship week and for themselves, having a wireless and speakers installed at school. By 1945 South Holmwood children had provided 30,000 cigarettes under the Cigarettes for Troops campaign.

An ex-pupil of the school, Dorothy Gardner, was awarded the George Medal in 1941. A twenty-three year old probationer nurse at the Royal East Sussex Hospital in Hastings she threw herself bodily over a frail patient during an air raid and was covered with debris so deep when the ward roof caved in that it took fifteen minutes to release her. The patient escaped with a bruised shoulder but Nurse Gardner's injuries were at first thought to be fatal for a long splinter had been driven through her skull. Even three months later it was not known whether she would live. On her recovery, however, she came in to visit her old school.

Another with a distinguished record was Ernest Heasman, who later bought the partially destroyed Holmwood Park. The son of a Holmwood tenant farmer who had gone into business, he generated vast sums for the war effort, raising several million pounds in one week to pay for the aircraft-carrier, Ark Royal.

Holmwood Station was also busy, largely because of its proximity to Schermuly's Pistol Rocket Apparatus Company in Newdigate. Schermuly's produced maritime distress signals and flares, rockets that sent up kites, aerials, and cables attached to parachutes or that that could be used to illuminate water; route marking bombs and target identification flares. During the war, when fifty or sixty wagons at a time would come into Holmwood station loaded with gunpowder and explosives, Schermuly's expanded from fourteen to fifty-five acres and employed 1400 staff.

The war brought thousands of people through the Holmwood who would otherwise never have known of its existence: Holmwood households offered lodgings to Londoners who had been bombed out of their homes; the Army taught tank driving on the Common and fond memories remain of the Canadians and their Nissan huts on Moorhurst Lane, of Genesta Heath entertaining them at Moorhurst and at Holmwood Park, of their drinking at the Holly and Laurel and their gifts of chocolate and coffee.

The later stages of the war brought German prisoners of war to the brickworks. Some formed ties with the community. When nine of them left the Holmwood in December of 1946 Amy and Doris Way received a letter of thanks for their kindness and for the generosity of their families. *(Dorking Museum)*

91

Throughout Holmwood institutions struggled to maintain some semblance of normality: the Foresters carried on despite the loss, in 1942, of Jack Worrow. North Holmwood sports club provided a game for members of the forces on leave and for the home guard and civil defence services, its new pavilion, which had been erected just before the outbreak with monies loaned by Mrs Morrish of Holmwood Lodge, central to the community. By 1944 it had become a point of honour that the debt be repaid by the war's end and in the last year of the conflict dances and other fund-raising events were being held, not for the war effort, but in anticipation of peace.

By this time aerial activity was much reduced but there were still incidents: in March 1944 a Junkers crashed into Holmwood Common near Blackbrook. Bombing with manned aircraft was about to come to an end, however.

In the run-up to the Normandy landings military equipment was parked all over the villages. Troops trained in Four Wents and Polish paratroops called upon local children to report suspicious characters. The D-day landings did not bring an instant end to terror from the air: in June 1944 a flying bomb passed over Spring Cottages and crashed at Abinger Bottom. With the advent of these pilot-less missiles alerts came day and night. Children took their midday meals in the shelters; families from Spring Cottages occupied them by night. On 22nd June the impact of a flying bomb brought down near the Old Croft broke windows half a mile away. A few weeks later another fell near Mill Bottom and an anti-aircraft shell exploded outside the headmaster's window. In July a bomb at Holmwood Corner damaged Spring Cottages, smashing locks and blowing in the doors at the school opposite. A military guard was put in place to prevent looting. Another destroyed the greenhouses at Grandon Lodge. It was estimated that 11 high explosives, 3 oil incendiaries and 500 other incendiaries fell on North Holmwood parish alone. Gradually, though, the allies advanced and as the rocket bases fell into their hands the attacks came to an end.

Finally, on the 8th of May 1945, it was over. Bonfires were lit outside Spring Cottages, at the observation post on Cow Green, at Mill Bottom and on the Common facing Church Terrace. Observers lit an enormous V on the football pitch in flares. St Mary Magdalene held a thanksgiving service and victory tea parties were held at the village hall, at Bentsbrook Road in North Holmwood and at Mid Holmwood.

'Tonight at midnight I stood on the school forecourt and saw the reflection in the sky, not as in the past war years of burning London from enemy bombers which have previously passed overhead, but of the lights of London at peace again,' wrote Mr Jay. *'After nearly six years thank God – the blackouts are down, the lights are shining freely from the homes of the countryside.'*

After the War – the rise of the road

Bond's pond before road widening. In the 1970s toxins from dairy silos polluted streams. Bond's pond was particularly affected. Children rescued fish there with nets as the fire service stirred the pond to oxygenate it. Even so, in 1976, smells from leakages at Redlands Farm were so bad that residents slept with their windows shut.
(Des Scutt)

In 1944 the Ministry of Works proposed that a new town, one of a ring around London, be sited at Holmwood. The idea came to nothing, however, Crawley being selected instead. Though the mood was one of optimism - despite it being impossible to purchase bats or balls until 1946 North Holmwood celebrated twenty-five years of cricket in its first peacetime season – times were hard. The winter of 1946 was a severe one. Food was in short supply and parcels came in from Rangiora and Tahri in New Zealand, from Ocean Grove in Australia and Huntsville in Canada. School attendance was low and heating erratic as coal supplies ran out. In January 1947 frozen toilets at South Holmwood School forced a two month closure and though a gas cooker and water heater were acquired the following winter heating remained sporadic there. As petrol came off the ration, however, the journey to school became dangerous once more. In June 1948 eight-year-old Patricia Entwistle was knocked down whilst crossing from Spring Cottages to school. A few weeks later Victor Salt of Moorhurst was knocked down near the station. By the 1950s, however, many children were passengers rather than pedestrians, being bussed to school when South Holmwood, like North Holmwood, became a primary school; at eleven children would either win a place at Dorking Grammar, or go to the secondary school in Beare Green.

In 1955 the Deepdene, (long in decline and headquarters of the Southern Railway during the war), was auctioned. (Amongst the lots were the freeholds to Inholms House and Cottage on the Blackbrook road, the White Barn (Ivy Porch), and North Holmwood Sports Ground: the club raised three hundred pounds to buy the freehold). In the same year the Duke of Norfolk severed his link with the ancient manorial estate.

The sale of Holmwood Common marked the end of the administrative system which had prevailed for nearly a thousand years. For decades complaints about bogs and blocked footpaths had grumbled on. During the war subscriptions to the Common Committee had fallen away, the Duke had stopped paying his share and the common keeper had been dispensed with. The post-war years saw huge changes in the landscape as the number of beasts grazed on the Common dwindled. Fewer households kept animals and the work done by horses was replaced with motorised vehicles. The advent of bovine tuberculosis in the 1950s made segregation of cattle necessary. With the end of communal grazing bracken, nettles and brambles thrived; hazel seeded itself; trees took root; views disappeared and footpaths could only be maintained by regular use. The Common reverted to dense scrub woodland, its formerly open views obscured. The Common required management and the chairman of the Committee, Sir John Dalton of Littlebrook, enquired as to the possibility of acquiring it. In 1953 the Duke announced his intention to sell. Two years later it was agreed that the three authorities having responsibility for Holmwood would purchase the Common and hand it to the National Trust. The County Council pledged half of the £5000 sale price leaving the Dorking Urban and Rural district councils to raise the balance.

Whether the acquisition was a legitimate use of public money was a contentious issue. Purchase and maintenance costs must be recouped from ratepayers but much of the benefit of acquisition would be enjoyed by outsiders. However in March 1954 Philip Henman, the retired businessman and philanthropist who farmed Folly Farm, pledged to pay the Rural District Council's share of acquisition and maintenance costs for the first three years. Lieutenant Colonel Mackintosh of Brookmeadow also pledged fifty pounds, gifts which were accepted with relief by councillors. On 20th September 1955 a ceremony to mark the handing over of the Common to the National Trust was held near the war memorial. A photograph appeared in The Times.

With Mackintosh's money paths were opened up, swamps drained and ditches put in; fire rides were cut and litter cleared. Bushes and brambles were cleared from around the Bell Holm Hotel giving views for two miles. Four Wents Pond, which had become so silted that angling was possible only with wader and nets, was dug out. (The six hundred fish found there were returned to the water). Similar operations were carried out at North Holmwood and Bond's ponds and in 1958 the Friends of Holmwood Common was formed.

The councils were represented on the National Trust's Common management committee; local residents were not. Nor was what the Trust planned always in keeping with local aspirations. In 1956 concerns over proposed car parks on the Common, particularly for one at the cricket ground, brought public meetings, locals fearing that Holmwood would become 'another Hampstead Heath'. The Trust also ran into opposition over recognition of commoners' rights. The Commons Registration Act required that these be registered in 1965 but proving their historical existence and that they were in use was not straightforward. Few had deeds setting out what had historically existed and whereas in the past those living next to the Common might point to the number of cattle or horses that they customarily kept there, by the mid-twentieth century commoners were faced with trying to prove what had until recently been grazed and which it could be assumed had been their right. Most claims were reduced to estovers and grazing for one or two horses, (many of the larger houses having continued to keep horses long after they had dispensed with other livestock). The law was not observed to the letter, however: the Commons Commissioner allowed the registration of rights with regard to ducks and chickens though only geese could in law be commonable, allowing them onto the register 'to promote harmony'. Time, however, has made even these obsolete; though more than thirty households have the right to do so, none of today's commoners grazes animals on the Common.

After the break-up of the Deepdene and Bury Hill came the demise of lesser estates. Many who had gone into the forces or into war work never returned - to Holmwood or to domestic service. The great houses which depended upon their labour deteriorated. Henrietta Pyke died in 1967 and with no demand for a mansion the size of Capel Lyse her house was demolished. Three smaller properties – New, Oakdene and Capel Lyse Houses – were built on the site. (Vigo remained in the family.) A similar fate befell the rest of the original Oakdene estate on the death of Bertram Watney in 1960 when Brookwood Corner was split from the remaining lands. By the 1970s it had been further broken down. Nor did Cuthbert Heath's son, Leopold Cuthbert, who inherited Anstie Grange on his father's death in 1939, ever occupy it. Queen Alexandra's Imperial Military Nursing Service continued in occupation until 1952 when the two hundred acres were auctioned in lots. Not a year later the adjoining family estate at Kitlands (comprising Anstiebury Camp, Minnickwood and Chasemores), was broken up by Leopold Cuthbert's cousin, Cuthbert Helsham Heath Caldwell. In 1971 Minnickwood was further broken down. Holmwood Park - partly broken up on the death of John Bruce Nichols in 1929 - was another victim. With the house partially destroyed what remained was sold separately from the estate lots in 1953.

The difficulty of managing without staff affected not just the mansions but the substantial family houses, many of which had been requisitioned during the war. Returning owners faced large costs to return them to family residences and with domestic help hard to obtain during the war even those that had remained in residential use had been neglected. The middle classes were looking to houses that could be managed with new technology and a minimum of labour. The sprawling piles of the Holmwood, with their pantries, larders, housekeepers' and butlers' rooms were unmanageable. Many of the Holmwood's finest never returned to family occupation.

They found other uses: Eutrie House became the research headquarters of Aircraft Steel Structures Limited, Daisy Lodge (Bellis House) a secretarial college, Holmesdale House a school and the Knoll the headquarters of the Waterisation Company Limited, a rust-proofing business. (It was later occupied by Biwater but eventually demolished.) In 1951 Oakdale was let to the London County Council for use as a children's nursery and illegitimate babies began to appear in St Mary Magdalene's baptismal registers with only their mothers' names recorded. From deprived backgrounds, many with learning difficulties or social and emotional problems, the children proved a challenge to South Holmwood School. By the 1960s the nursery was used by several London boroughs for the under fives. Because of its remoteness, however, the home was always difficult to staff and by the end of the decade, with social mores and attitudes to poverty changing, the difficulties of visiting the infants in a property so far from their homes was recognized and the nursery closed.

Even the church could not provide for its incumbents to the standard of times past: Rev Spurway, who became vicar of South Holmwood in 1947, was the last to enjoy the splendour of the great vicarage. In 1960 he made national headlines when he employed a Canadian fundraiser at a fee of £1000 to boost the church's income. One parishioner was quoted in the Sunday Pictorial: *'It's like selling God door to door'*, to which Mr Spurway replied: *'People expect the church to be here when they want a wedding or a funeral or a christening. Well it just won't be here unless they pay to keep it here.'* In 1967 the stables were demolished and the vicarage, in a deplorable condition, was sold. It became Foxmead Residential Home.

The demand was for smaller properties of the type that, with the

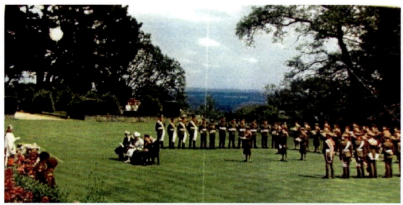

Queen Mary listens to a military band in the grounds of Anstie Grange in 1947. She was there to present awards to recruits at Queen Alexandra's Imperial Military Nursing Service Headquarters. *(Nursing Times)*

development of Chart Downs and Goodwyns Farm, were spreading towards North Holmwood. By the 1950s service directories were treating that area as a suburb of Dorking, and a noisy, industrial suburb it was. Not only did the road drive through it, with transport cafes and goods yards at the top of Spook Hill, but the brickworks was much expanded. By the 1960s fifteen million bricks a year were being produced there. Oil-fired kilns fired smuts over the vicinity, causing burns and ruining clothes, the smell so obnoxious that windows had to be kept shut even in summer. A local doctor contended that the health of children was being affected and that there were increased cases of bronchitis. Not surprisingly, when Holmwood Lodge, the gardens of which were edged by the vast site, came up for sale in 1969 it was demolished. St Johns Road, Lodge Court, Eccles Hill, North Close and the Orchard now occupy the site.

Nonetheless, North Holmwood was busy and prosperous. The nearby Sports Association and its pavilion continued to provide a focus for social life. Though cricket remained central ladies' stoolball and netball sections had been formed during the war. Boys competed at cross country and girls at athletics. There were hopes of a netball court and of a football pitch. In 1948 a Sussex eleven played a benefit match at the ground in aid of Harry Parks and John Landgridge; Eddie Watts lead out an eleven the following year. There was annual excitement when the London Evening Standard landed its helicopter at the ground on

Industrial North Holmwood

Holmesdale Road - the entrance to the brickworks that was once the road to Stubs Farm.
In the 1960s an extension of the works across farmland south of Inholms Lane was proposed and in 1968 a concrete batching plant was planned to which a vehicle a minute would require access. The plan was vociferously opposed by residents who claimed that they were already suffering cracks in their walls because of brick lorries and that they could not leave windows open for dust. Protest meetings were held, followed by a public enquiry. To the relief of residents the plan was rejected.

The brickworks supported a number of trades and industries in the vicinity and the whole North Holmwood area was dotted with yards, depots and transport cafes. Next to Arlington Cottage beside the Cabin was Sim's yard (left). (The site is now occupied by bungalows.) Benson's yard, at the top of Spook Hill, remains.
(Dorking Museum/Des Scutt)

the way to Goodwood. Guests at club dinners at the Watermill included radio commentators and Surrey players. By the 1960s, however, the pavilion was showing its age, necessitating a new round of raffles, sponsored walks and barbeques.

Having been discontinued during the war at South Holmwood, cricket was also re-established when cessation of hostilities freed up the pitch, and it was here that the commentator, Christopher Martin Jenkins of the Dutch House played in vacations as a boy.

The post-war world, with its welfare state, social mobility and increased opportunity, was a changed one. The Foresters were in decline. By 1963 so few people were attending that meetings were no longer quorate, (though 90 people attended the Holmwood court's centenary dinner at the Windmill in 1969). The Norfolk and the Foresters, their fates so entwined for nearly a hundred years, were strangely timely in their demises. The Norfolk, like the Holly and Laurel, was suffering from the lack of its traditional travelling trade. Car passengers stopped less frequently than charabanc or coach parties. People took their holidays further afield and wayside businesses felt the loss. When the Brook House Hotel by Grandon Lodge burned down the plot was sold for housing. The last Foresters' meeting at the Norfolk was held in December 1969, after which the hotel closed on the illness the landlords. It never re-opened. The Foresters limped on a little longer, meeting at the house of Stan Pierce but in 1971 the High Court of the Foresters passed a resolution governing the structure of courts with less than fifty members. Though the committee resisted amalgamation with another court, in the end they had no choice.

Just as the Holmwood Foresters were finding their identity eroded, the Norfolk community found itself recognised for the first time. After a petition by the Holmwood Women's Institute in 1971 the area between George's Tea Bar at the top of Spook Hill and the Norfolk was given a name: Mid Holmwood. The Council also formalized road names in the area. It proposed that the track leading to Littlebrook and Brookmeadow be known as Mid Holmwood Lane. Holmwood View Road and Brook Valley, (which name had been in use since the beginning of the century), were agreed for the other roads to the east of the A24. On the western side Oaks Lane, Norfolk Lane, Bond's Lane and Swallow Lane were decided upon for the tracks leading into the Common there, the suggestions of Isemongers Lane and Goose Green, (after the geese once found at the Norfolk), being rejected. At North Holmwood residents objected to the proposed designation of Holmesdale Terrace for the houses opposite the post office. Instead it became Willow Green – after the willows lining the paths there. Maintenance of these lanes and others running to isolated dwellings within the Common remained a matter for the landowner, however, a thorny issue since the advent of mass car ownership had caused some, like Mid Holmwood Lane, to deteriorate badly.

Flooding at Mid Holmwood in 1968. The car is that of champion rally driver, Dave Pierce - another of the family that has been in business in Holmwood, (at the Norfolk Arms, in the building trade, at the Norfolk Garage and at Pierce and Street Motors), since Charles Field Pierce came to the inn in the 1860s. *(Des Scutt)*

Increased car ownership meant diminished railway use. Trains had been crowded in the late 1940s, (as on the 6th of November 1947 when a Holmwood to London train collided in fog with the Waterloo to Chessington south-bound train at Motspur Park killing four people). By 1959, however, passenger services had been

By the 1960s the Norfolk Garage had become a full-scale petrol station. *(Des Scutt)*

reduced to seven a day. The Dorking to Horsham route was marginalised as Gatwick took over as the hub for the south-east. In 1964 the goods yard closed; coal henceforth came into the Hoads' depot by road. In 1968 the roof to the bridge over the line was removed.

As far as roads were concerned, however, the Holmwoods remained very much on the main line. The Hoads' Holmwood Garage was not short of trade, nor Frank Pierce's Norfolk Garage. As more Holmwood residents acquired cars, the more a car became necessary, the old isolation of the Holmwood returning for those without their own transport: in 1967 the parish of South Holmwood bought a small bus, running it with voluntary drivers to convey people to the village as buses became less frequent.

But the A24 was neither wide nor straight, and traffic, which had often been heavy in pre-war years, was, by the late 1950s, more than the road could accommodate. Queues to and from the coast in the summer grew long and were often stationary, local children going out to watch the chaos as cars crawled nose to tail on their weary way. By the late 1960s the chaos was not confined to weekends and rush hours. Hardly suitable for the volume of traffic now using it, the road that had brought the villages into being, now began to undermine them. The solution to the problem, however, would tear the heart out of the villages.

The Great Train Robbery – the Holmwood connection

On August 16th 1963 two bags of banknotes were found in Redlands Wood by a man and a woman on their way to work whose motorbike had overheated. Police with dogs found a further briefcase and suitcase. All appeared to have been abandoned in a hurry, with little attempt made to hide them. When counted at Dorking Police Station by staff of the Midland Bank the stash was found to amount to £101,000.
Part of the haul from the robbery of the Glasgow to London mail train in Buckinghamshire a week previously, (during which £2 ½ million had been stolen), it was never established at the subsequent trials of the perpetrators why the money was brought to Holmwood or by whom though several of the robbers lived or originated close by – at Redhill, East Molesey, Ashtead and East Horsley. Though two of the bags belonged to Brian Field, who had purchased the group's headquarters, it was established at trial that he had not deposited them. Holmwood is on the road to the coast, however, (and another stash was found in a caravan on Box Hill), where other gang members had headed with their hoards. One writer has alleged that the mystery is explained by the involvement of persons who were never charged.

The Lost Villages

Work began in 1966. One option was to widen the road along its entire length. Running a dual carriageway through North Holmwood, however, would have required the demolition of numerous houses. Instead it was decided to build a new stretch across Holmwood Farm. This left the farm isolated from the village. It also left a wedge of land sandwiched between Spook Hill and the new carriageway which became home to Dorking's fire and ambulance stations. At Mid Holmwood the widening separated the dwellings on the eastern side of the Common from Bond's store and the Norfolk. It also required the demolition of the annexe to the Bell Holm Hotel. At South Holmwood the cricket ground was obliterated and the village sliced in two, Spring Cottages cut off from the church and school. Further south the road cut a new course across Breakspeares and Bregsells, (the track leading out to Bregsells being routed under the elevated carriageways). The station was left in a backwater.

Holmwood Farm house was demolished. Parts of several gardens, of the Norfolk and of the garage, were also requisitioned. On the northbound carriageway George's Tea Bar at the top of Spook Hill became inaccessible to half its customers. Its owners put in a planning application for conversion into a petrol station. Facing a total loss of trade in what had hardly been an idyllic location for some time, the owners of the Bell Holm did likewise, claiming that the only viable alternative was a truckers' stop. Both applications were refused. The hotel was demolished.

Fast traffic now passed within feet of those houses at Mid Holmwood that had been discreetly set back from the road, the residents on one side no longer able to commune with those on the other. Though the council looked at proposals for a bridge there nothing materialised. At South Holmwood the Holly and Laurel and the Sundial faced a dual carriageway rather than a green square. The heart had been torn out of the villages.

Life, however, went on. In 1974 North Holmwood celebrated a hundred years of the parish with a flower festival and a cricket match played to 1874 rules. Three years later South Holmwood celebrated the Silver Jubilee with a street party, 'It's a Knockout' competition, barn dance and barbeque, which plans did not differ greatly from royal celebrations of generations past. The spirit of community had hardly been swept away.

Nonetheless, it was not what it had been. Social and geographical mobility now took people who might once have spent their lives in Holmwood elsewhere. One such was the son of Pedlar Barnes, who had made his living from the Common, gathering moss and herbs supplemented by grave-digging: from the grammar school in Dorking he became the first person in Britain to graduate in the Chinese language. Conversely,

Work begins on the new carriageways over Holmwood Farm. *(Dorking Advertiser)*

The end of the Bell Holm Hotel

BELL HOLM HOTEL

(Licensed Hotel and Restaurant)

NORTH HOLMWOOD

Nr. Dorking, Surrey

Phone: Dorking 73227

Situated in lovely countryside on edge of National Trust Land, in two acres of lawns and gardens.

All bedrooms fitted with Hot and Cold basins and Fires. Central heating

We are particularly well-known for our good cuisine.

Conveniently situated for London and the coast, both by rail and road.

TARIFF

Bed and Breakfast from 21/-

Four or more days from 30 - per day.

(Not applicable to Bank Holidays)

WEEKLY TERMS ON APPLICATION

Above prices subject to 10% service charge.

Previously The Elms, the hotel was lost to the dual carriageway. The depiction of its destruction in the local press heralded the coming of the great new road, but the holiday business in Holmwood was in any event on the wane. *(Des Scutt)*

almost universal car ownership brought people into the Holmwood who no longer need live close to their work, their mobility allowing them to enjoy the countryside without the disadvantages of isolation. Demand for housing within reach of commuter destinations grew and property prices rose. Though farms still surrounded the Common by the 1970s most Holmwood dwellers made their livings in Dorking, Leatherhead, Guildford or Reigate, or commuted up to London. Those few who made a living from the land were soon unable to afford the prices properties on and about the Common could now command.

Nor was there much of a living to be made from the Holmwood's traditional business of servicing the needs of travellers. Drivers on the dual carriageway sped by without stopping for refreshment or provisions. The Holly and Laurel closed, leaving the villages without a public house. Attempts to establish a pizza restaurant and tearoom on the site also failed. Even the Little Chef at Mid Holmwood, which was built to provide a quick stop for the traveller, failed. The only remaining hostelry is the Plough at Blackbrook.

By the late 1970s locals did not even shop in the villages. Garman's closed in 1979. In the same year the Worsfold brothers closed the post office that their parents had taken over from the Crofts. It became Holmwood Tyres.

A new cricket pitch was established at South Holmwood behind the war memorial but it was never satisfactory. Cricket is no longer played there but in North Holmwood the Sports Club has transformed itself into something akin to a village pub and hall in one *(Des Scutt)*

Hamlin's the grocer closed, as did the Dawes' fruit and vegetable stall. At Mid Holmwood Bond's was no

100

more and Frost's of North Holmwood became a hair salon. By the end of the century there was but one convenience store in North Holmwood, one in Beare Green, and Barker's next to the Holly and Laurel. Even the family-run Holmwood and Norfolk petrol stations were seen off by competition from outside the villages.

Rail services also diminished. With Horsham travellers preferring the faster Gatwick services the Horsham extension to the Dorking line was only attractive to residents of the villages between the two towns. In 1986, therefore, with reduced services and Holmwood commuters driving into Dorking to get the train, the station buildings were demolished. Now the station is unmanned, its platforms troubled by trains only once or twice an hour at certain times of the day.

With increased mobility came centralisation. With the coming of the new Redlands primary, built on what had been Goodwyns Farm, North Holmwood School closed its doors and in 1994, despite protests, the school started by Charlotte Larpent over a hundred and fifty years earlier followed suit. The North Holmwood schoolhouse remains in community use; it became the village hall after a fundraising campaign. In South Holmwood the school buildings were converted into residential accommodation.

Such was also the fate the Hoads' yard on Warwick Road, the Holmwood Garage and the White Hart. The greatest of these transformations, however, was at the North Holmwood brickworks where production ceased in 1981. The Holmwood Park estate was built on the site soon afterwards. With the scar of the brickworks gone and housing running up to Chart Downs, North Holmwood became a quiet Dorking suburb on a pretty willow-shrouded green.

Business premises might have been disappearing but those of Holmwood's large houses that survived into the 1980s were less likely to be pulled down than in previous decades. Anstie Grange, Mill House and Oakdale were instead split into apartments. Ironically, though, many of their cottages, coach-houses and lodges, sold off with plots of garden, were too small for modern tastes, necessitating conservatories and extensions.

Few Holmwood residents now take from the Common more than a few blackberries, sloes and some holly. Nor do many make their livings within the villages. Businesses survive, however, which have their origins in those traders who serviced the turnpike: Holmwood Tractors at the Norfolk Garage carries on the motor trade that superseded landlord Taylor's horse vehicles. Opposite the name of Taylor's predecessor at the inn is maintained in Pierce and Street, the mechanics who operate from next to the Norfolk Villa to which Charles Field Pierce and his wife Susannah retired when he gave up the inn more than a hundred and twenty years ago.

In the twenty-first century the Holmwood remains distinct. Planning regulation and the ownership of the National Trust have prevented its being subsumed into the suburbs of Dorking, the Common left an island. Still surrounded by its farms the Common retains more

In July 1976 an argument over change on the dodgems lead to the fatal stabbing of North Holmwood's Tommy Benson on Clapham Common. Benson's fairground rides had long occupied the yard at the top of Spook Hill. *(Dorking Museum)*

or less the outline of 1649, pockets of development in and around it following patterns that were set down four hundred years ago. Estates have come and gone but the boundaries of individual plots often follow the field and farm boundaries of four centuries ago. It looks very different however, even from fifty years ago. Only active management prevents scrub, bracken, brambles and hazel obscuring paths to create dark, dense woodland in which few species of plant or animal could survive. Even the ponds require maintenance: in 1995 a new dam and bridge were put in to North Holmwood pond and in 2000 Four Wents was drained and cleared.

The Common may no longer play a part in the agricultural economy but its wildlife has not reverted to what it was before man's intervention; the flora and fauna of the English countryside has changed. Pheasants originating from the Caucasus and China and Mandarin ducks, the descendents of escapees from wildfowl collections, are as likely to be seen as native species. Badgers, foxes, rabbits, and a large population of roe deer reside on the Common. Adders and grass-snakes, frogs, toads and newts can also be seen and there is a colony of Daubenton bats at Four Wents whilst elsewhere the pipistrelle inhabits crevices in trees. The Common is also home to a variety of bird life, even the nightingale, which used to be frequently heard in the Holmwood's coppices and mature hedges. The uncommon oak hook tip moth and the brown hairstreak butterfly live on the blackthorn and the Common is the only lowland site in the country where the weevil Procus granulicollis has been recorded.

Part of the old brickworks, gifted to the Woodland Trust by Wimpey Homes, is also a haven for nature. Lying between the new houses and Inholms Lane, there are no signs advertising its informal paths but it is designated a site of Nature Conservation.

The centuries have seen the brickworks site go from woodland to farmland, to brickworks and back to woodland on a journey not dissimilar to that of the Common. But whilst the demand for clay, for grazing and for arable land has declined, the demand for housing shows no sign of abating. A few small encroachments within the Common have come and gone, all evidence of them disappeared; most have steadily grown. As yet Holmwood has managed to remain distinct from the town to its north, retaining a sense of community and a definite character despite the assaults of rail and road technology; it remains to be seen what the future will bring.

Holmwood's stars of the screen –

Bill Travers and Virginia McKenna

The actors and wildlife campaigners Virginia McKenna and Bill Travers lived at Gamekeeper's Cottage in Anstie Lane, once part of the vast Heath estates. In 1966 they starred in 'Born Free', the film of the lives of George and Joy Adamson and their lioness, Elsa, afterwards founding the Born Free Foundation. George Adamson stayed a month with them in Holmwood in 1984. Another star of the screen, Jonnie, the springer spaniel who appeared in 'Ring of Bright Water', lived with them in Holmwood.

'Sweet' Mary Millington

Dark glasses hide the grief for Diana Dors. By her side is her actor husband Alan Lake.

Stars attend Mary's funeral

Mary's initials, made from pink and white carnations, by her graveside.

ACTRESS Diana Dors was among 150 mourners at the funeral of blue movie queen Mary Millington at South Holmwood Parish Church on Friday.

She and many others wept as the small coffin was lowered into the ground in front of two huge capital M's made of pink and white carnations. Mary was put in the same grave as her mother Joan Quilter, who died just over two years ago.

Mary's husband Bob Maxted was supported by friends as he stood by the grave. Her only other relative at the funeral was a cousin.

Earlier the Rev Patrick McNeice had conducted a simple, short service with no hymns.

Bouquets of flowers for Mary stretched across the small graveyard, glowing with colour in the bright sunshine.

By one was the message: "To Mary –

Bloom new in God's garden, Our love will always be with you."

Mr Maxted's message, with red roses, said:

"To Mary – we miss you already, we will never forget you. All our love, Bob, Reject and Tippi (the couple's dogs)."

Flowers were also sent by animal groups Mary had helped including some from the Hastings PDSA.

Supporters of the National Campaign of the Obscene Publications Act described Mary as a "freedom fighter" in a card they sent.

Several former neighbours of Mary's from the time she lived in the village, joined in paying their last respects.

● More pictures page 3.

'or youth

URTEEN new part-time uth workers have been ointed in the Surrey Central ucation Area.

Widow dies in crash

A 73-year-old Beare Green widow died in a

Mary Millington, (born Mary Ruth Quilter), moved from London to Woodlands View in Mid Holmwood with her mother as a child. She worked as a waitress at the Bell Holm Hotel and married local butcher's boy Bob Maxted. Always sexually liberated and renowned locally for her skimpy bikinis and sunbathing topless on the Common, she was spotted by a glamour photographer and modelling lead to an extremely successful career in the porn industry. Her best known film was the 1977 'Come Play with Me'.

Even at the height of Mary's success she and her husband were still living with her mother, to whom she was devoted, in Mid Holmwood. She was well regarded in the village and though she drove expensive cars and travelled extensively many locals did not know her profession until a Canadian fan let the cat out of the bag at the pub. Suffering addiction and depression on the death of her mother, Mary committed suicide in 1979 at the age of thirty-three. Soho sex shops and pornographic cinemas closed on the day of her funeral at St Mary Magdalene where she was buried alongside her mother. 150 mourners, including Diana Dors and her husband, attended and bouquets were laid out in rows across the churchyard where a swarm of journalists interviewed locals about 'Sweet Mary' for the national papers.

In 1999 a biography, 'Come Play with Me; The Life and Films of Mary Millington', was published by Simon Sheridan. (*Dorking Advertiser*)

Select Bibliography and Sources

Abbreviations

DLHG   Dorking Local History Group   DM   Dorking and District Museum
SHC   Surrey History Centre   NA   National Archives
AC   Arundel Castle Archives   Surrey Arch Coll Surrey Archaeological Collections

General Sources

Arundel Castle Archives: manor of Dorking surveys, accounts, court rolls, maps and other documents
Dorking Museum: maps, transcripts of court rolls, sales particulars, poor rate books, directories and
Surrey Domestic Buildings Research Group reports
Surrey History Centre: maps, censuses, tithe records, parish registers and poor rate books

Minute books, committee papers and accounts:

Ancient Order of Foresters, Holmwood Court 1912-1976 SHC 7374/3/1/1-3; Beare Green Prosecuting
Society 1823-1890 SHC 898/4/1-80; Beare Green Prosecuting Society Committee Minute Book and
Annual Meetings 1825-1889, Accounts 1823-1889 and Minutes Books 1890-1916 DM SC.R/15;
Capel Village Hospital Committee 1866-1933 SHC 2915/1; Holmwood Common Committee,
Minutes of Meetings of the General and Sub Committees 1883-1891, DM R.43/1; Holmwood
Defence Committee, Dorking and District Area (Defence of the Realm Act) 1914 – 1916 SHC
898/4/1-80; Holmwood Fire Brigade Committee Minute Books 1909-1921 SHC HO/11/3; Holmwood
National School Minute Book 1869-1897 SHC HO/12.2; Dorking Police Occurrence Books, 1838-40
SHC (awaiting cataloguing); Minute Book of South Holmwood Church Building Committee, 1862
SHC HO/7/2; Parish Council Minute Books, Rural Dorking area 1894-1901 SHC P 18/1/1; South
Holmwood King Edward VII Coronation Memorial committee minute book 1902 SHC HO/11/1;
South Holmwood Coronation Celebrations 1937, correspondence and accounts SHC 2064/5; South
Holmwood Coronation Committee Minute Book 1911 SHC HO/11/2; South Holmwood School Log
Book 1872-1961 SHC 2064/1/1-4; South Holmwood Church Committee report on Mrs Helsham
Jones' Legacy SHC HO/7/4; Waywardens Minute Book 1881-1888 SHC P 18/2/1; estate of Mr
Rohde Hawkins, 1884 SHC 6627/1; John Marten, Butcher, South Holmwood, 1718 SHC 1376/1;
Surveyors of the Highway Account Book 1775-1822 SHC P 18/3/1; Dorking and District Refugee
Committee papers DM R.63; Horsham and Dorking Turnpike Road Account book 1847-1853 SHC
414/3/29; North Holmwood School records of Walter Piper, Headmaster 1882-1924, DM 155/1&2;
Overseers of the Poor Minute Book 1895-1913 SHC P 18/2/1; Papers re Holmwood National School
252 1873, Charitable Trusts Act NA Ed 49/7376; awards for bravery awarded June 1941 NA T336/32;
re Hope: De Cetto v Hope 1894-1913 NA J91/166; Charity Commissioners re scheme for Holmwood
School NA ED 49/7380; Westminster Council re Oakdale Nursery 1964-70 NA BN 62/2491 and
2492; Ministry of Agriculture re farms on Holmwood Common 1941-2 NA MAF 32/1048/41 and
25/1048/141; Dorking Rural District Council Private Streetworks Act 1892 records DM R.36/3;
papers relating to proposed enclosure of the commons of the manors of Dorking and Shellwood AC
M944, AC FC 150 and AC MD 2342

Correspondence:

Lord Farrer of Abinger to the Society for Preservation of Commons 1911 SHC 2572/34/1; Holmwood
Boy Scouts and the War Department 1941 SHC HO/14/3; sale of Liquor at South Holmwood Village
Hall SHC HO/13/8; Sir Leopold Heath and the ornamentation of South Holmwood Church 1901 SHC
HO/7/3; Rev. Wickham and Cuthbert Heath re the attribution of a picture in Holmwood Church SHC
HO/7/6; AP Wickham to Mr Cole regarding his mother's memorial SHC HO/7/10; Swan family and
Holmwood Windmill DM SC.5/15/1- 20; Mary Ann Arnold to Rev P Beath re establishment of a new
parish SHC CAP/17/3; prisoners of war at North Holmwood brickworks DM R.306

Deeds:

Brookmeadow and Brookmeadow Cottage; Littlebrook Farm (SHC 248/10/1-35); Holmwood
Windmill (SHC 2676/83/17, 18); Mission Room (SHC HO/7/2, 20); Swires estate (SHC 933/1);
Warwick Road and Norfolk Road (SHC 4326/1); Kitlands and Minnickwood estate (SHC 6537);

Inholms House (SHC 7392/3/1); Holmwood Park DM R.66; Grandon Lodge 1858 SHC 4414/1/124;
Langholm Cottage, 1906 197/4/8-15; Inholms Farm AC D4439-4451 & AC STD 110; Holmwood
Farm and Martyrs AC MD 805 & AC FC 357

Other:
Survey of the Manor of Dorking 1649, copied and updated 1753 SHC 196/2/2
Epsom and Dorking Turnpike Act 1755
Documentation relating to the formation of the ecclesiastical Districts of Holmwood and Coldharbour
        SHC HO/9/1-6; Order in Council re the formation of Coldharbour Parish 1848 SHC 1591/1
Grant Approvals and Church Plans, Lambeth Palace Archive
Surveyors report to Duke of Norfolk on survey of 1838 SHC 436/7&8
Plans for a new Parsonage house at South Holmwood 1839 SHC 472/17
Plans for school buildings in South Holmwood 1844 SHC 264/22/1-13
List of seatholders at South Holmwood Church 1914 SHC HO/7/11
Bertha Broadwood Nursing report 1884 SHC 2185/1/1
Return of Licensed Houses and Beer houses, Dorking Petty Sessional Divisions 1892
        DM H.176/6; Victualler's Registers 1786-1826 DM H.176/5
South Holmwood Drainage Contract Tender 1900, DM R.36/2
Dorking Brick Company order books SHC 7324/1 & 6845/11; correspondence SHC 6845/9;
        employment registers DM
Dorking Congregational Church Refugee Register 1940-44 DM R.68
Diary of Beatrice E Kynaston 1939-1945 DM R.30/1
Home Office Aliens Department: Internees Index NA PRO H/O 396/63/216 & 396/80/344
Location Statement 7th Battalion Surrey Home Guard DM R.115/1
Captain Pinckney's papers and weather logs from Sunnyside 1953-1971 DM R612/1/1/27 & 613/1-3
Street Survey 1975-1982, Dorking Local History Group
North Holmwood Over-60s Club Scrapbooks DM R.590/1-4
Notes on the Stilwell family DM R.276
A Scrapbook of the Holmwood – Women's Institute, 1949 DM HOLM
Surrey and Sussex Aviation Society, Press Release 1976 DM H210

Newspapers and Journals
Dorking Advertiser, Surrey Advertiser, Votes for Women, The Times, The Daily Mail, Church Times,
Country Life, The Spire, The Dorkinian, Nursing Times, Sunday Pictorial, Lutyens Society
Newsletters, London Gazette, Holmwood Parish Magazine 1891-1914, 1942 SHC 40/18/4, Morning
Herald; Redland News; Newspaper Cutting Collection DM 3028/7

Select bibliography
Anon, *Walks, Rides and Drives around Dorking*, 1866
Arigho, Bernie: *Twentieth Century Holmwood*, 2000
Attlee, John: *Reminiscences of Old Dorking 1850-1860*
Atherton, Kathy: 'The Admiral and the Obnoxious Ornaments', *Dorking History* (DLHG), 2007
Atherton, Kathy: 'A bit of singing and dancing: Emmeline Pethick Lawrence, the Esperance
        Girls' Club and the Sundial', *Dorking History* (DLHG), 2006
Atherton, Kathy: 'The Evacuation of the Holmwoods', *Dorking History* (DLHG), 2005
Atherton, Kathy and Worrow, S.E.: 'The Norfolk Arms, Holmwood', *Dorking History* (DLHG), 2004
Barnes, Archie: 'Memories of Holmwood', *The Dorkinian*, 2003
Bastien, F.: 'Daniel Defoe and the Dorking District', *Surrey Arch Coll* Vol.55, 1958
Bird, Joanna: 'Notes on a Romano-British Clasp Knife from North Holmwood', *Surrey
        Archaeological Collections,* Vol.84, 1997
Bird, Joanna and Bird, D.G.: *The Archaeology of Surrey to 1540,* 1987
Bonner, Arthur: 'Surrey Place Names', *Surrey Archaeological Collections,* Vol.37, 1926
Boucher, C.T.G.: *John Rennie 1761-1821*, 1963
Brandon, Peter: *A History of Surrey*, 1998
Brandon, Peter: *The Kent and Sussex Weald,* 2003

Brandon, Peter: *The North Downs*, 2005

Brayley, Edward Wedlake: *A Topographical History of Surrey*, vol.5, 1848

Bright, John S.: *A History of Dorking and the Neighbouring Parishes*, 1884

Brittain, Vera: *Pethick Lawrence, a Portrait*, 1963

Brown, Anthony: *Cuthbert Heath, Maker of the Modern Lloyds of London*, 1980

Brown, John W.: *Highways & Byways in Dorking*, 1909

Brown, John W.: *A Victorian Guide to Dorking*, 1852

Brown, John W.: *Black's 1861 Guide to Dorking*, 1861

Camden, William: *Britannia – Surrey and Sussex*, 1586

Cobbett, William: *Rural Rides*, 1830

Cole, Maureen: 'The Holmwood Manoeuvres of July 1876', *Dorking History* (DLHG), 2007

Cole, Martin and Maureen: 'The Oakdene Estate, South Holmwood', *Surrey Gardens Trust Newsletter*, spring/summer 2004

Collier, A.C.: *The Story of North Holmwood Church*, 1974

Cotton, David: 'A Short History of the Holmwood', *St Mary Magdalene Parish Magazine*, 1970

Defoe, Daniel: *A Tour Through the Whole Island of Great Britain*, 1724

Dennis, John: *Illustrated Handbook of Dorking*, 1858

Dent, John: *The Quest for Nonsuch*, 1962

Dinnage, William Henry: *Recollections of Old Dorking*, 1977

'Downsman': *Rambles in Surrey*, 1947

Ettlinger, Vivien, Jackson, Alan A., and Overell, Brian: *Dorking, A Surrey Market Town Through Twenty Centuries*, 1991

Ettlinger, Vivien, Gower, John, and Green, Lionel: 'Stane Street at North Holmwood' *Surrey Archaeological Society Bulletin*, No 195, 1984

Farries, K.G. and Mason, M.T.: *The Windmills of Surrey and Inner London*, 1966

Fordham, Peta: *The Robbers' Tale*, 1963

Godwin- Austen, R.A.: 'Anstiebury Camp', *Surrey Arch Collections*, Vol.5, 1871

Gover, J.E.B., Mawer, A., and Stenton, F.M., with Bonner, W.A.: *The Place Names of Surrey*, 1969

Green, F.E.: *The Surrey Hills*, 1915

Green, Lionel: 'Church Spires and Major Rohde Hawkins', *Dorking History* (DLHG), 2000

Gosling, John and Craig, Dennis: *The Great Train Robbery*, 1964

Hale, Cecily: *A Good Long Life*, 1973

Hall, Alan: 'Investigation of Stane Street at South Holmwood, near Dorking', *Surrey Archaeological Collections*, Vol.91, 2004

Hamilton, Genesta: *A Stones Throw*, 1980

Harding, Keith: *Dorking Revisited*, 1997

Harrod, John T.A.: *Up the Dorking*, Southern Railways Group, 1999

Holland, Coffey: *Dorking People*, 1984

Jackson, Alan A.: *Dorking's Railways*, 1988

Jackson, Alan A.: 'The Cabin, North Holmwood', *Dorking History* (DLHG), 2003

Jackson, Alan A.: 'On the Buses around Dorking', *Dorking History* (DLHG), 1995

Japp, A.H.: *Dorking and Neighbourhood - A Handy Guide to Rambles in the District*, 1881

Kenney, Annie: *Memoirs of a Militant*, 1924

Knight, David: *Dorking in Wartime*, 1989

Lang, Cecil Y., and Shannon, Edgar F., jr ed.: *The Letters of Alfred, Lord Tennyson Vol. I 1821-50*, 1982

Malden, H.E.: *A History of the County of Surrey*, Part 25, Wotton Hundred, London 1911

Malden, H.E.: 'Kitlands in Capel', *Surrey Archaeological Collections*, Vol.28, 1915

Malden, H. E.: 'Notes on some Farms in Capel', *Surrey Arch Collections*, Vol.33, 1920

Malden, H.E.: 'Holmbury Hill and the Neighbourhood', *Surrey Arch Collections*, Vol.17, 1902

Malden, H.E.: 'An Eighteenth century journey through Surrey and Sussex', *Surrey*

Archaeological Collections, Vol.29, 1916

Malden, H.E.: 'Notes on Anstiebury, Holmbury and other Early Camps in Surrey', *Surrey Archaeological Collections,* Vol.12, 1894

Manning, Owen and Bray, William: *The History and Antiquities of the County of Surrey,* 1804

McCall, Albert: 'Bus Services from Dorking', *London Bus Magazine,* 1975

Meakings, C.A.F.: *Surrey Hearth Tax 1664,* Surrey, MCMXL

Miles, Walker: *Field-path Rambles comprising Routes round Dorking, Leith Hill, Holmwood, Wotton etc.,* 1894

Mitchell, Vic and Smith, Keith: 'Southern Main Lines', *Epsom to Horsham,* 1986

Mountford, Frances: *A Commoner's Cottage,* 1995

Mountford, Frances: 'Nathaniel Wix, an 18th Century Dorking Worthy', *Dorking History* (DLHG), 1990

Newbery, Celia, Ed.: *A History of Sport in Dorking,* 1985

Overell, Brian: 'Mrs Brown's Favourite Sculptor*', Dorking History* (DLHG), 1999

Overell, Brian: 'The North Holmwood Pottery', *Dorking History* (DLHG), 2002/3

Overell, Brian: 'A Missing Trust Deed', *Dorking History* 18 (DLHG)

Overell, Brian: 'More about the Prosecution of Thieves', *Newdigate Society Magazine no.39* R.409

Palmer, Pam: 'The Double Life of a Capel Yeoman', *Dorking History* (DLHG), 2007

Pethick-Lawrence, Emmeline: *My Part in a Changing World,* 1938

Pethick-Lawrence, Frederick: *Fate Has Been Kind,* 1943

Robinson, David: *The 1851 Religious Census: Surrey,* Surrey Record Society, 1999

Rose, Charles: *Recollections of Old Dorking,* 1878

Ruddock, Ted: *Arch Bridges and their Builders 1731-1835,* 1979

Rush, Chris: *South Holmwood in the 1920s and 1930s – unpublished DM*

Skempton, Professor Sir Alec: *A Biographical Dictionary of Civil Engineers Vol.1,* 2002

Smith, Bill: *A Tribute to a Great Lady and Two Great Gentlemen,* 1987

Smith, Bill: *The Holmwood, A Surrey Village – A History over 2000 Years,* 1982

Smith, Bill E.: *The Holmwood and District no.2,* 1983

Smith, Bill: *Down Memory Lane, Beare Green and the Holmwoods,* 1987

Smith, W.: 'The Holmwood Village Fire Brigade 1930', *Vigiles (Fire Brigades of Surrey Preservation Trust),* October 1988

Stiff, Neville G.J.: *The Church in Dorking and District,* 1912

Tarplee, Peter: *A Guide to the Industrial History of Mole Valley,* 1995

Thompson, F.: 'Three Surrey Hill Forts: Excavations at Anstiebury, Holmbury and Hascombe 1972-79', *The Antiquities Journal of London,* 1979

Timbs, John: *A Picturesque Promenade Round Dorking in Surrey,* 1824

Trotter, W.E.: *Select Illustrated Topography of Thirty Miles Around London,* 1839

Howard Turner, J.T.: *The London, Brighton and South Coast Railway,* London, 1979

Van der Lande, Charles: *Iron Age Hill-forts in Britain: Structures of Aggression of Defence,* Dissertation, 2003 DM R.530

Vanderbilt, Alfred Gwynne: *Mr AG Vanderbilt's Brighton and London Coach,* 1908

Walker, TEC: 'The turnpike to Guildford and Horsham', *Leatherhead Proceedings,* Vol.2, No.16, 1966

Winbolt, S.E.: *With a Spade on Stane Street,* 1936

Winbolt, S.E. and Lowther, A.W.G.: 'Notes on Stane Street in Redlands Wood, North Holmwood', *Surrey Archaeological Collections,* Vol.44, 1936

Womersley, Julian: *The Surrey Union Hunt,* 2007

Voysey, Robert T.: *Voysey's Rural Rambles,* 1932

Index